WATERDROP WATERDROP

COLORING BOOK EDITION

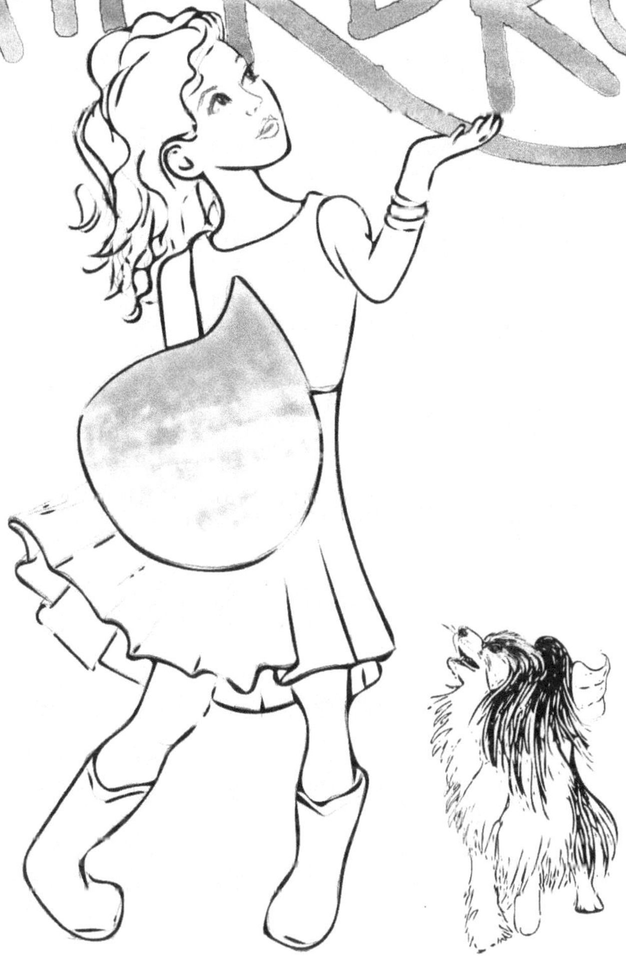

BY LORI JO MAGANA   ART BY PHYLLIS DILLARD

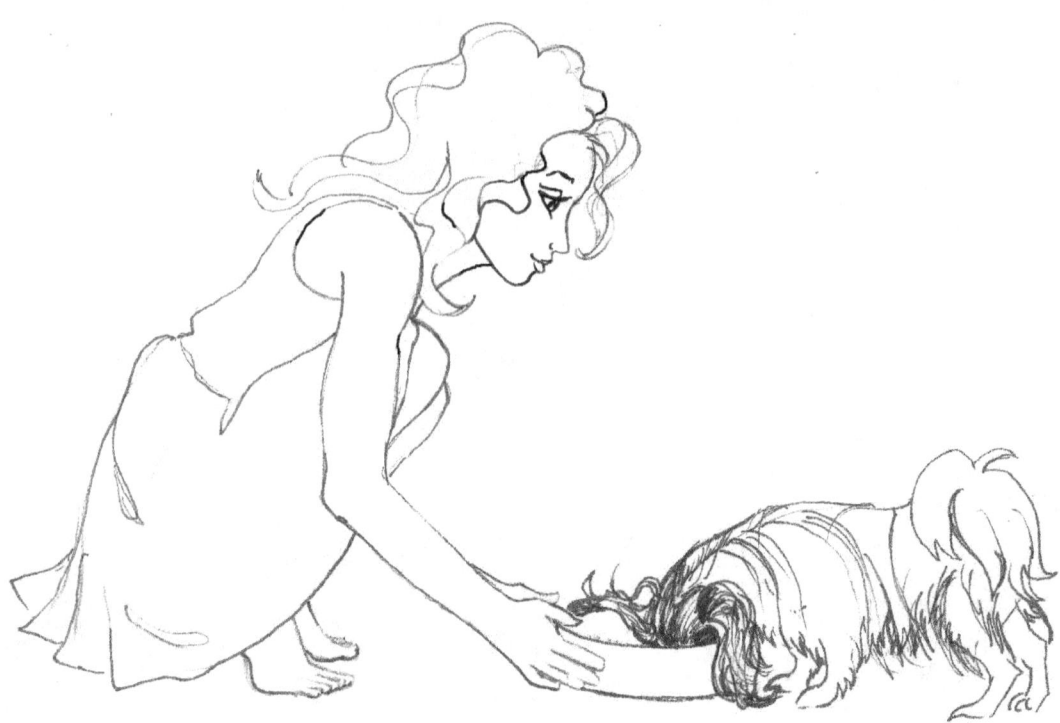

Copyright 2016 by Lori Jo Magana
Waterdrop, Waterdrop
The Coloring Book Edition

ISBN-13: 978-1535111065
ISBN-10: 1535111062

Visit us on the web by searching:
The Cookie Lobbyist
or
Word Spigot Publishing

Printed in the USA

WORD SPIGOT PUBLISHING
—————————————————
GEORGIA VIRGINIA OHIO

Dedicated to the memory of
The Frenchman
who loved the sunshine,
the mountains,
and the West Virginia rivers.

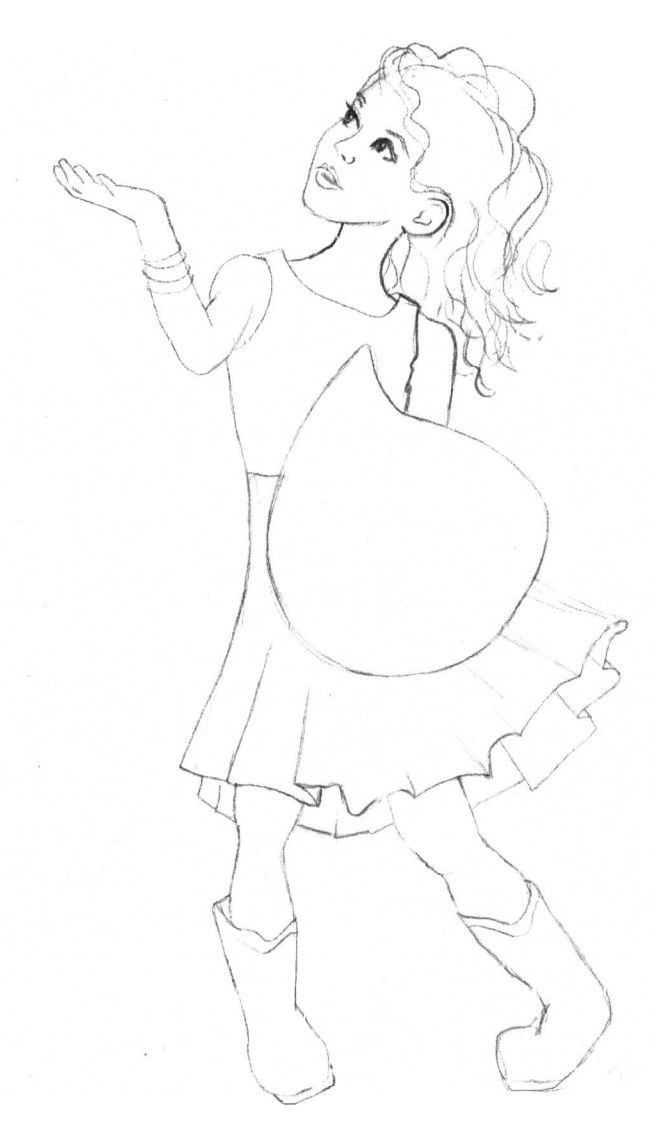

"Après la pluie, vient le beau temps."

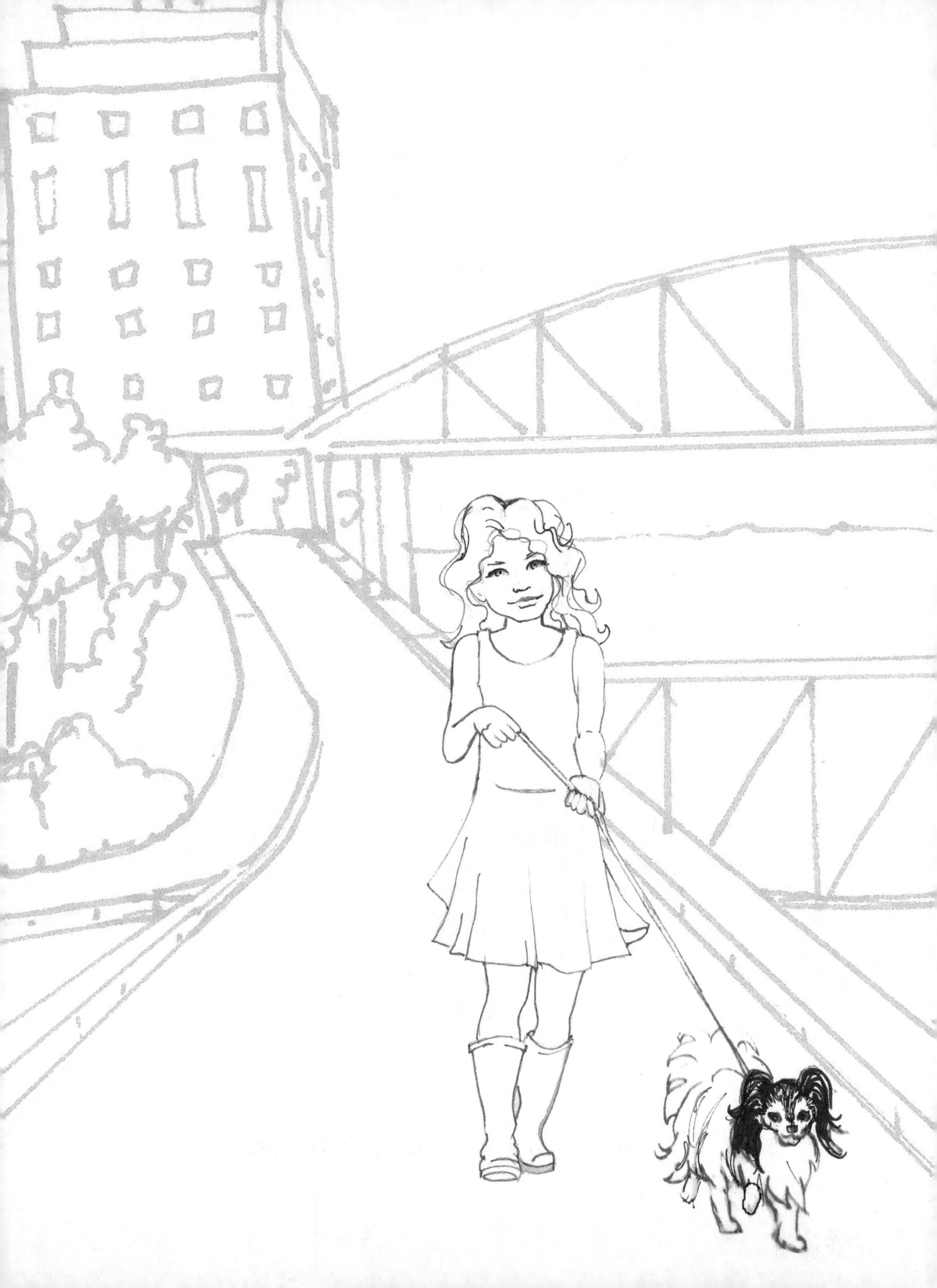

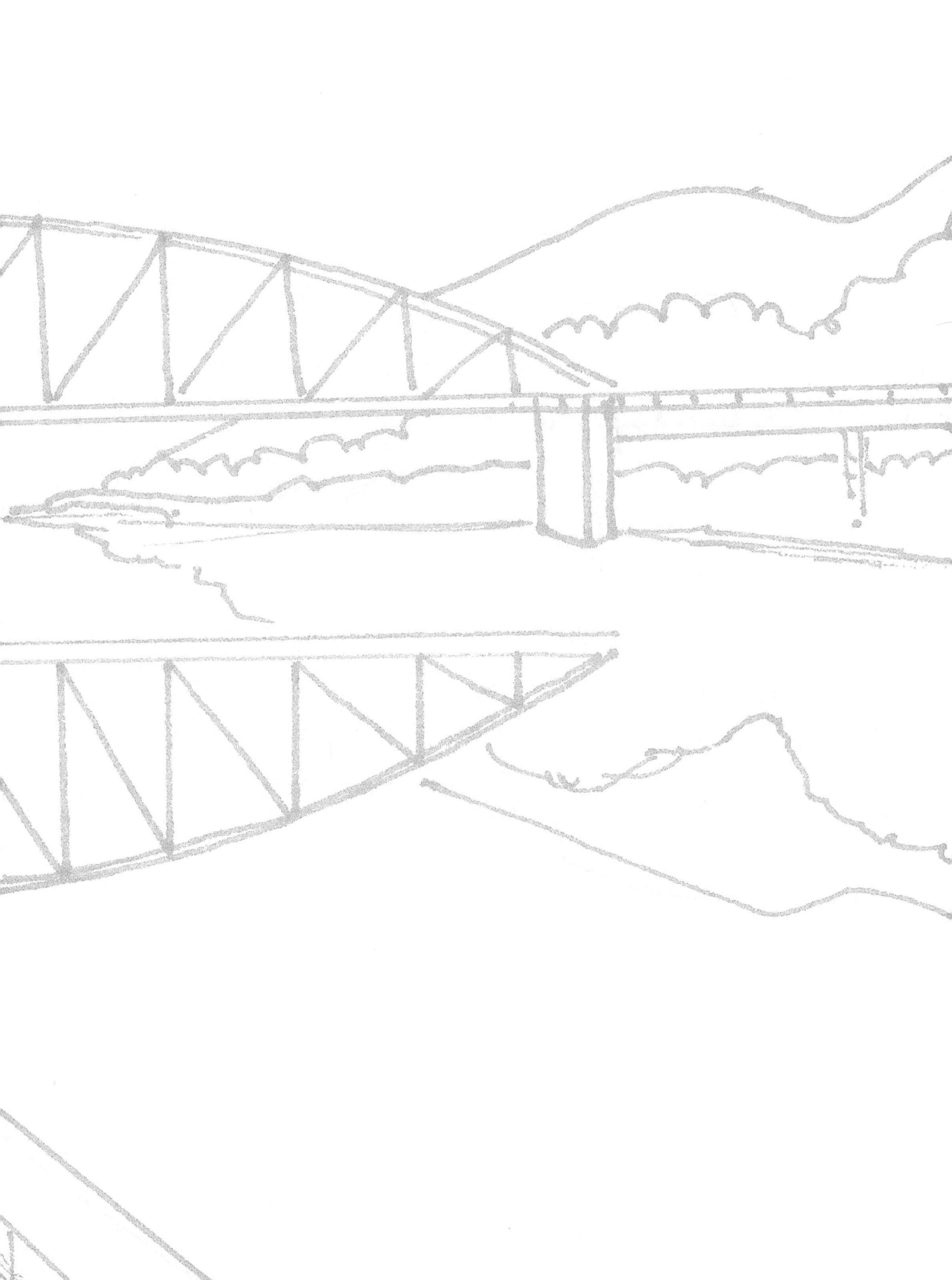

PROTECT OUR WATER

SIGNED:_____

PROTECT OUR WATER

SIGNED:_____

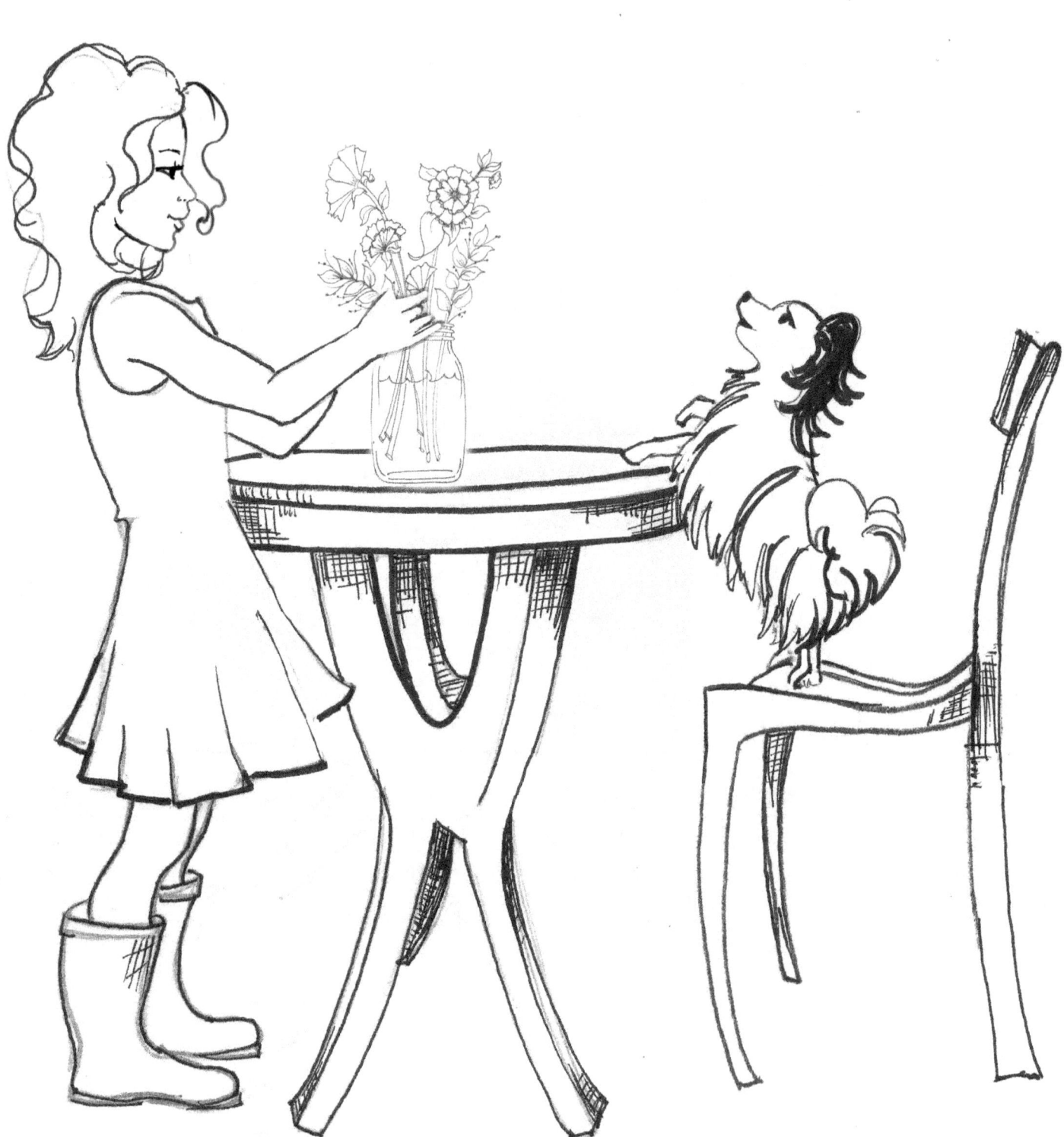

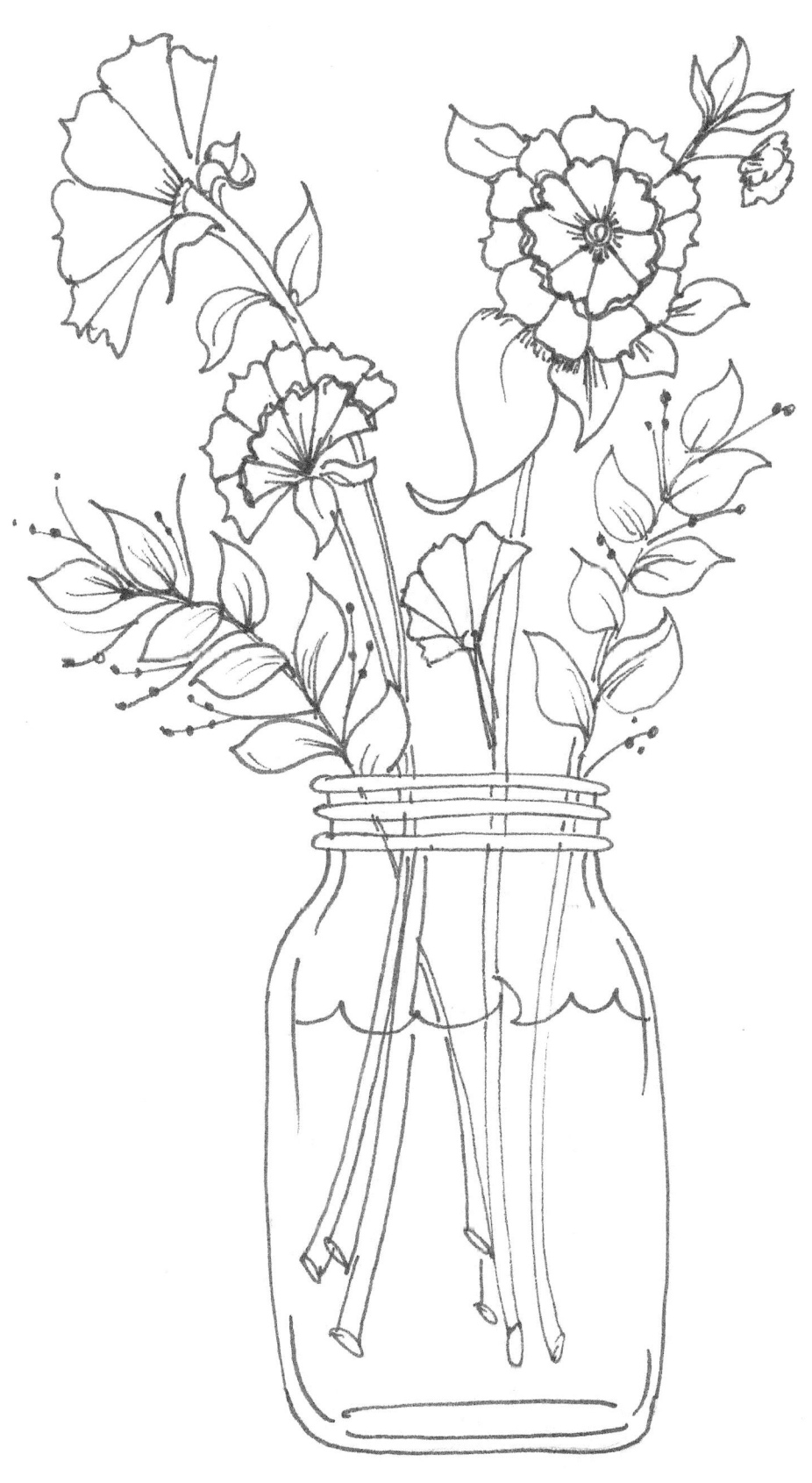

PROTECT OUR WATER

SIGNED:_____

PROTECT OUR WATER

SIGNED:_____

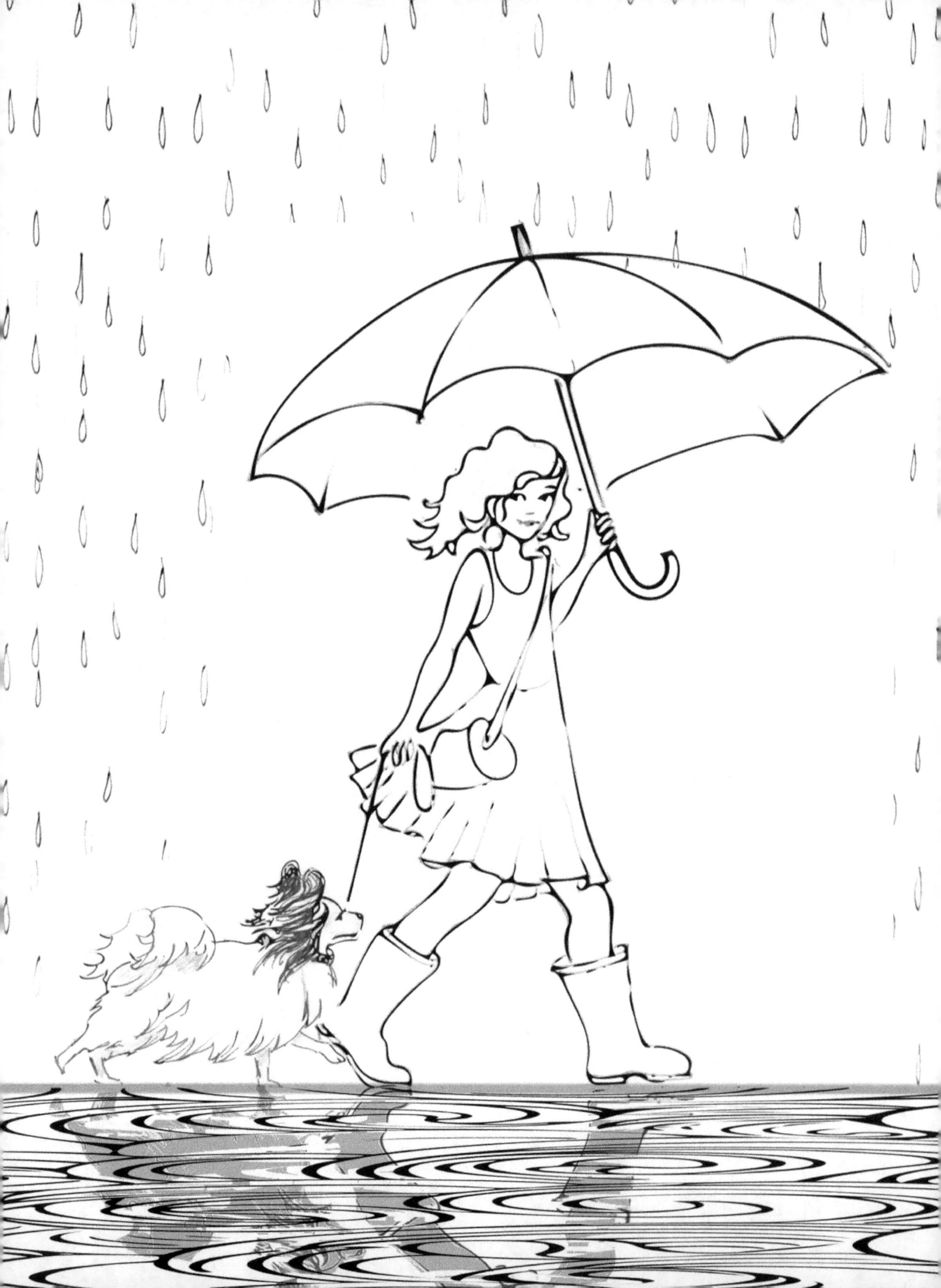

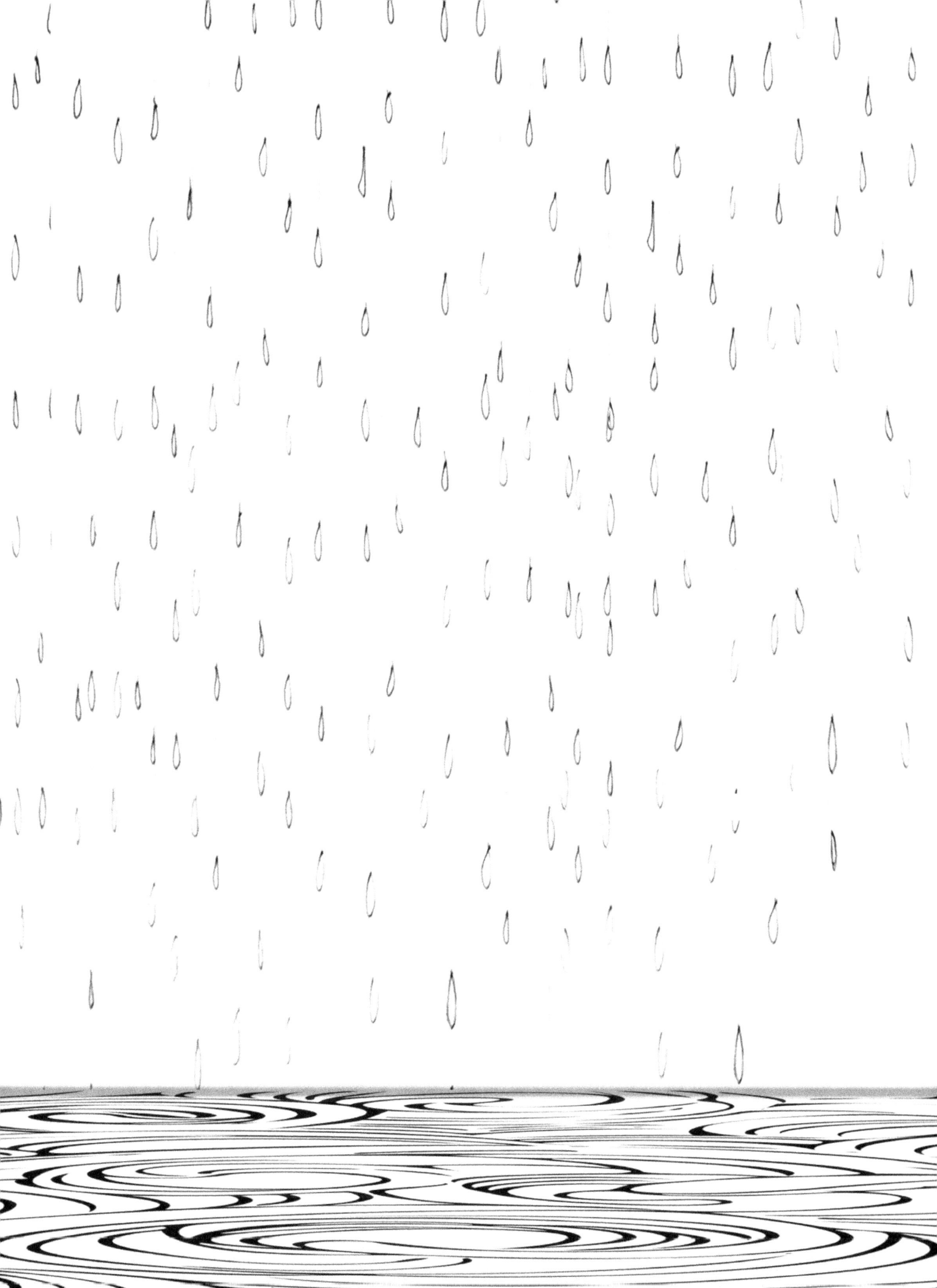

PROTECT OUR WATER

SIGNED:_____

PROTECT OUR WATER

SIGNED:_____

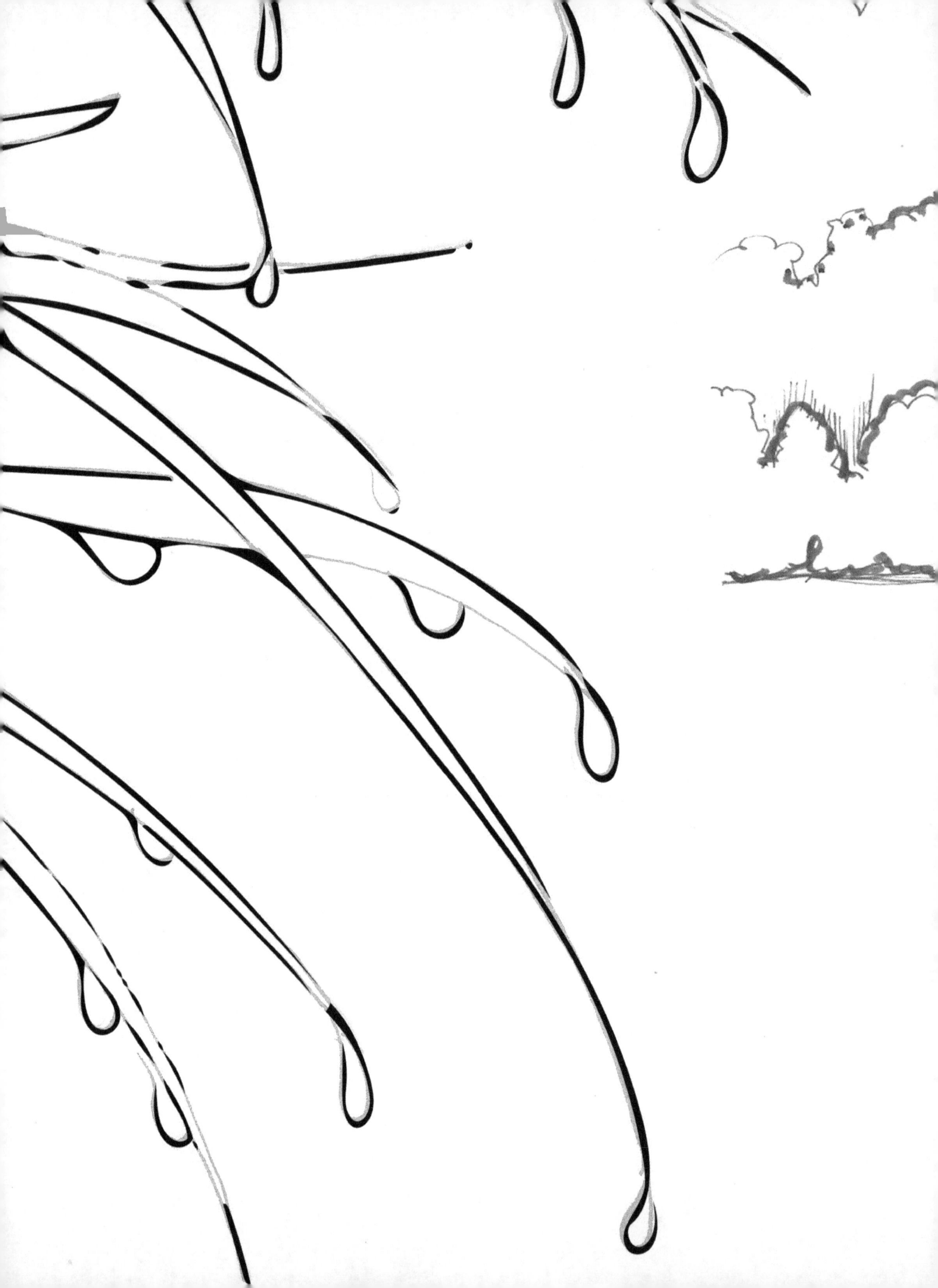

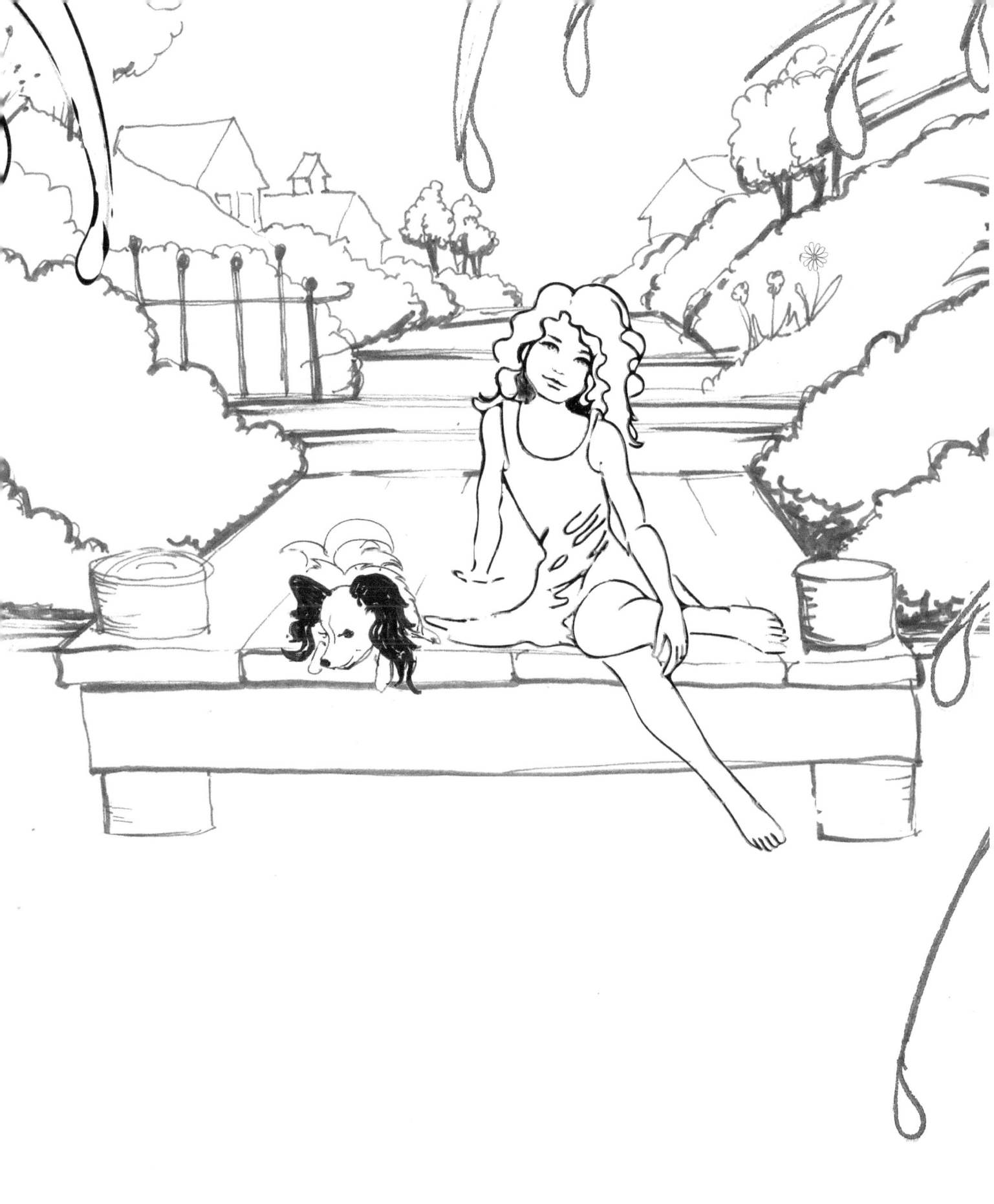

PROTECT OUR
WATER

SIGNED:_____

PROTECT OUR WATER

SIGNED:_____

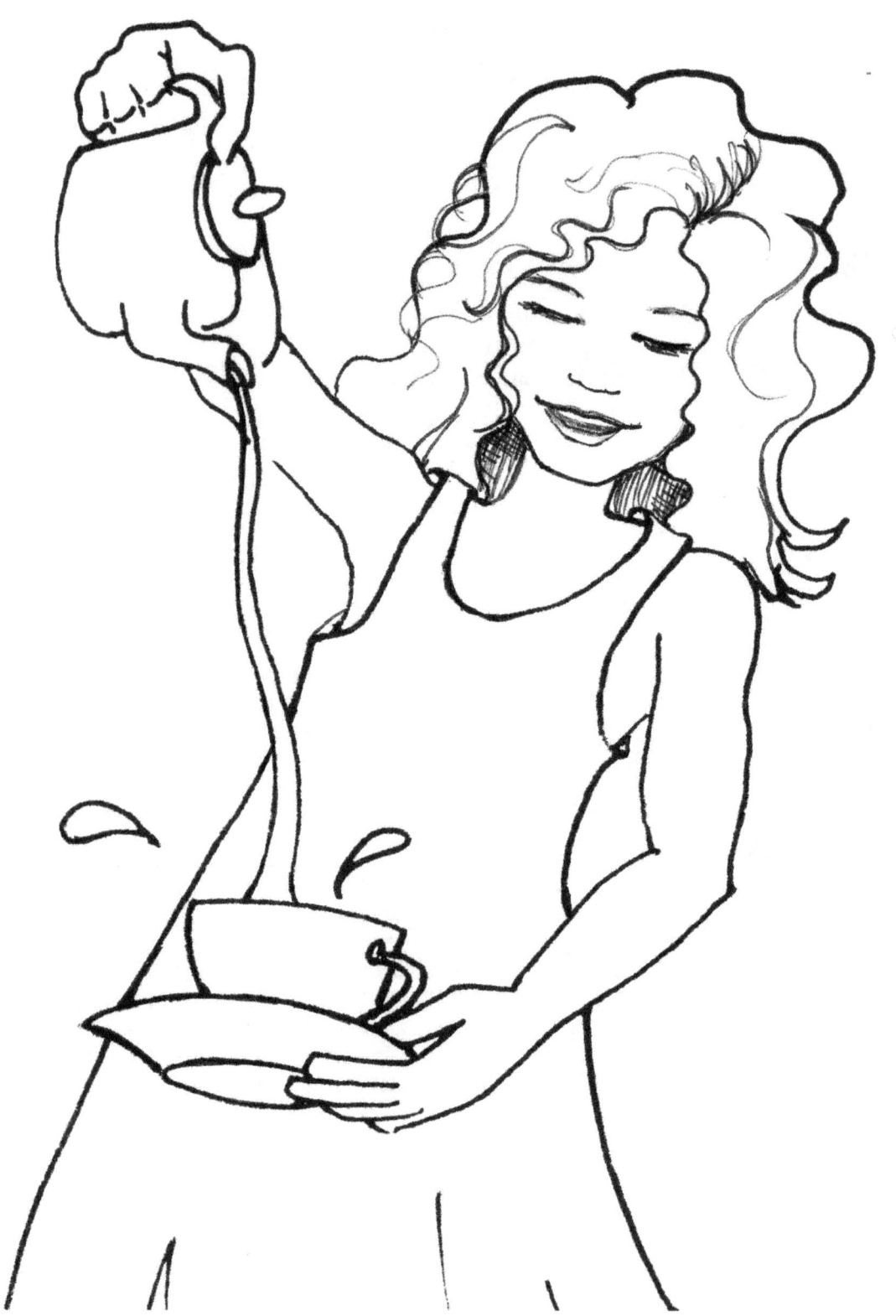

ME & WATER

100% –

70% –

0% –

PROTECT OUR WATER

SIGNED:_____

PROTECT OUR
WATER

SIGNED:_____

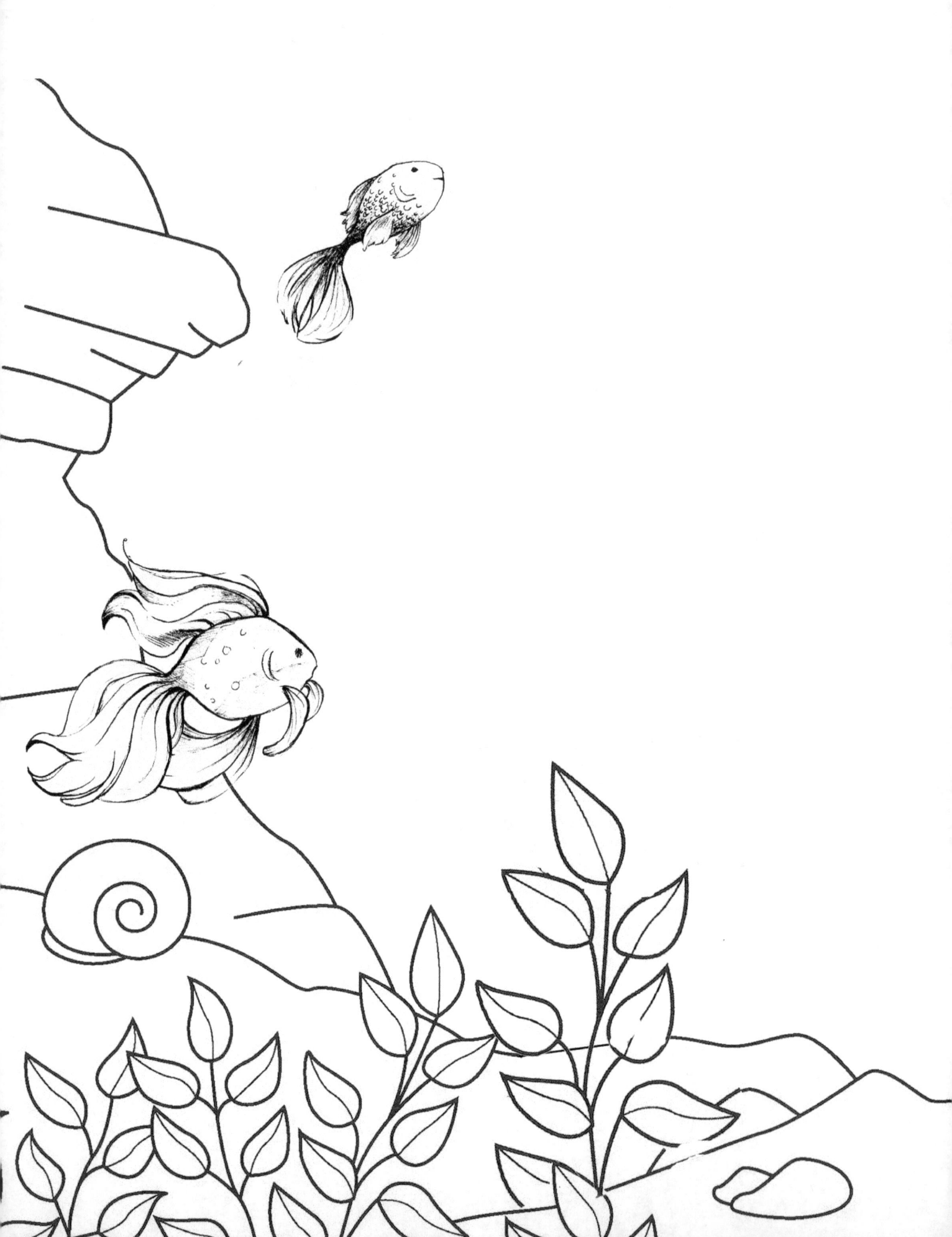

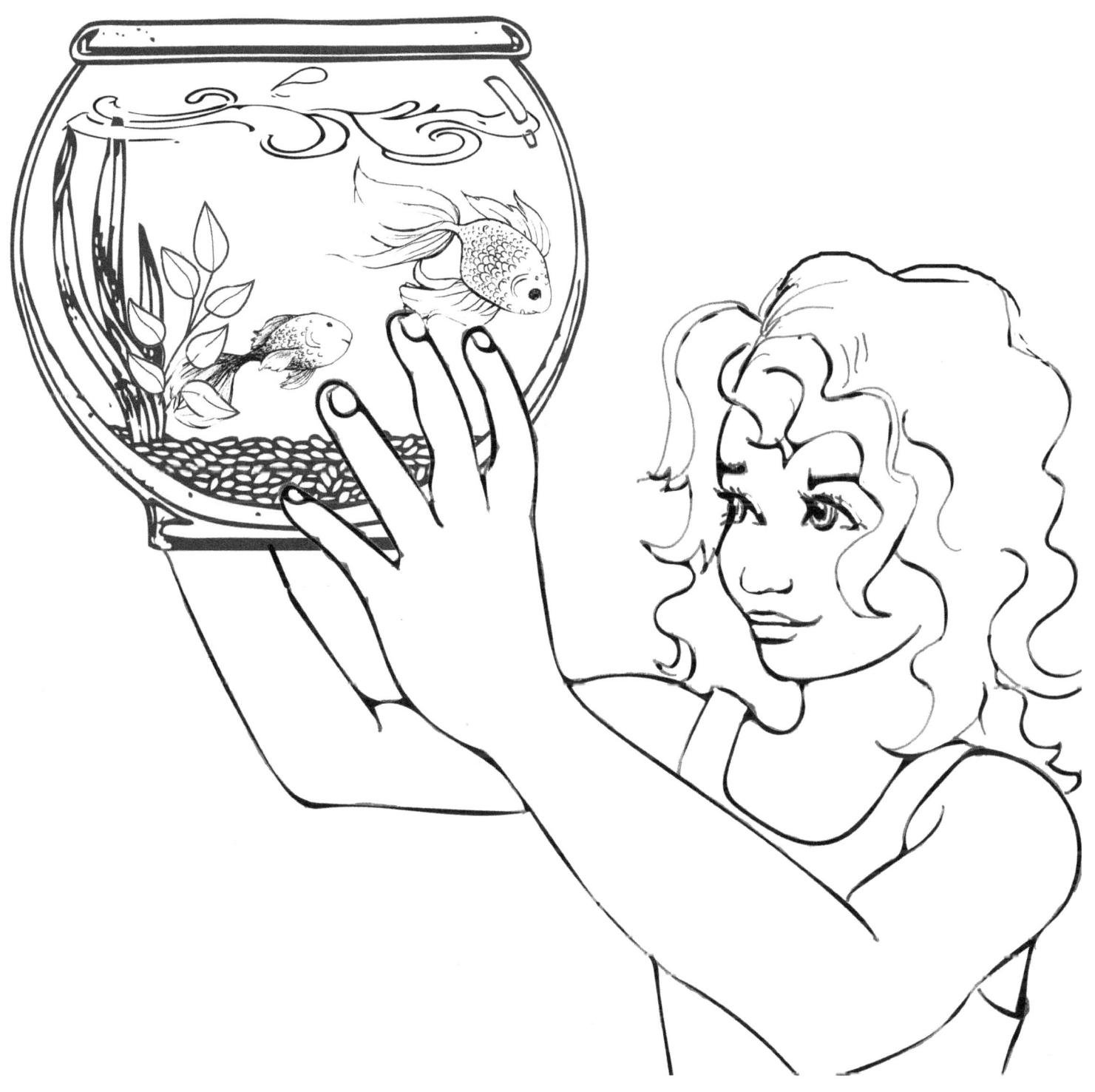

PROTECT OUR WATER

SIGNED:_____

PROTECT OUR
WATER

SIGNED:_____

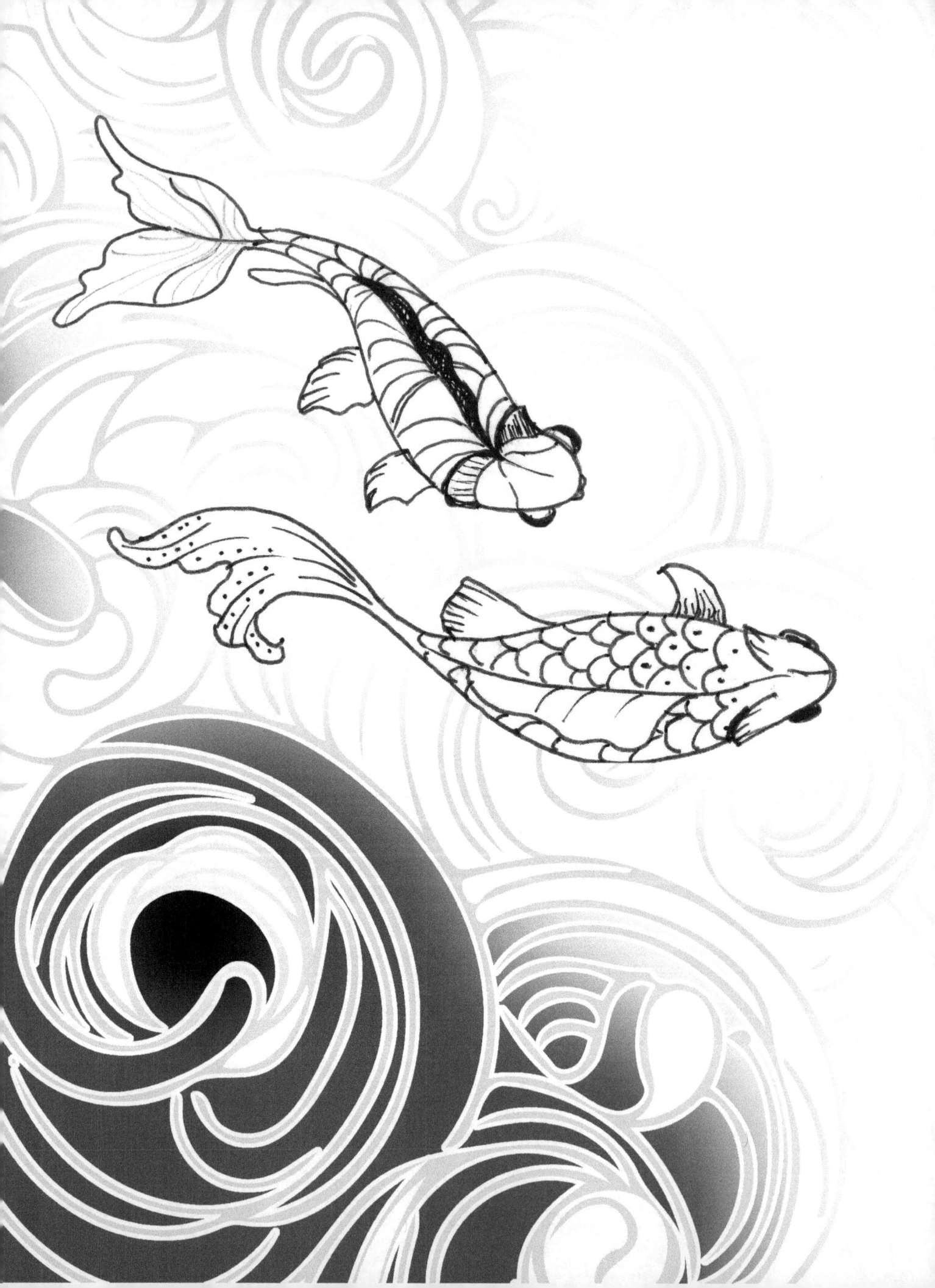

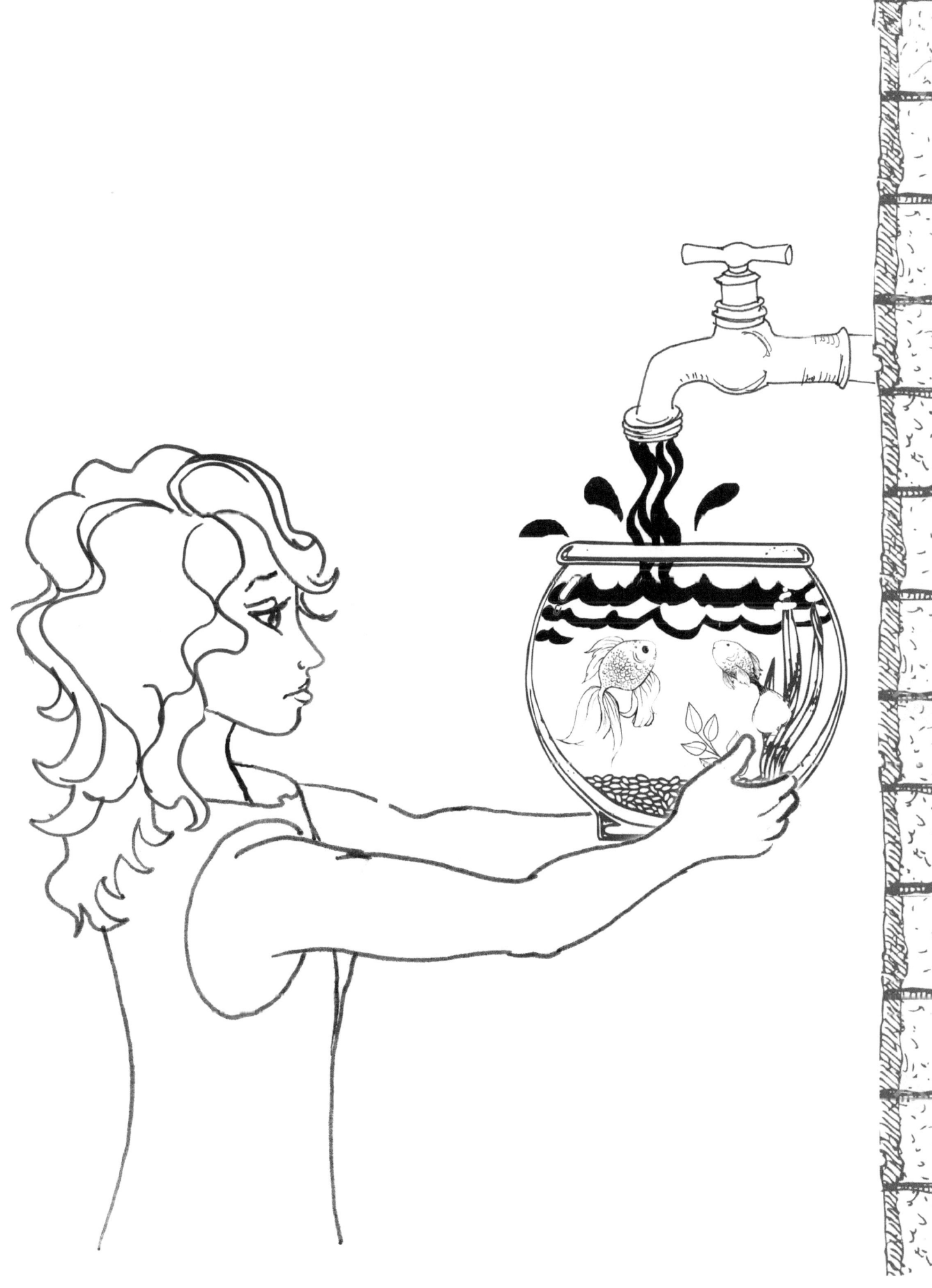

PROTECT OUR WATER

SIGNED:_____

PROTECT OUR WATER

SIGNED:_____

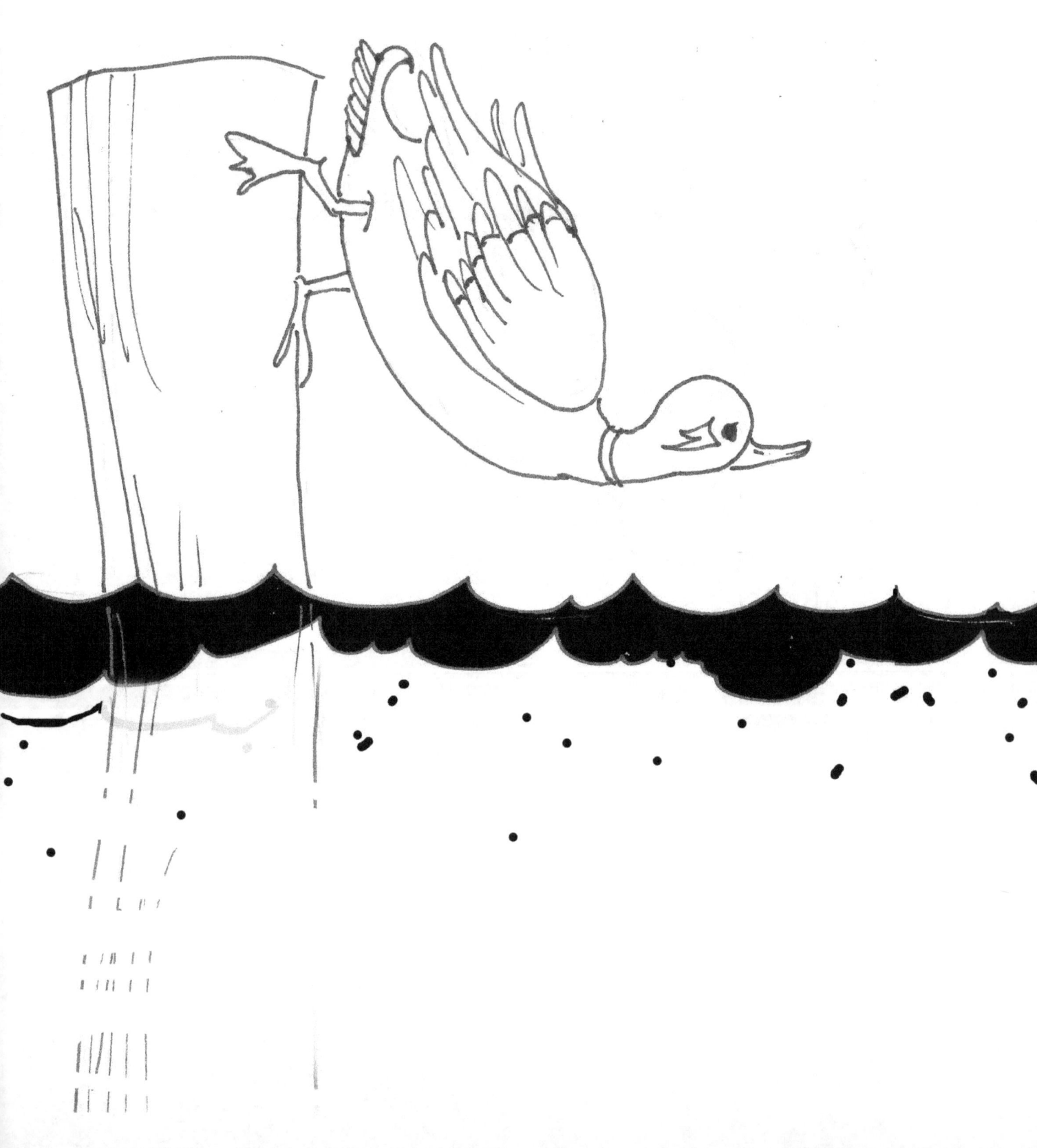

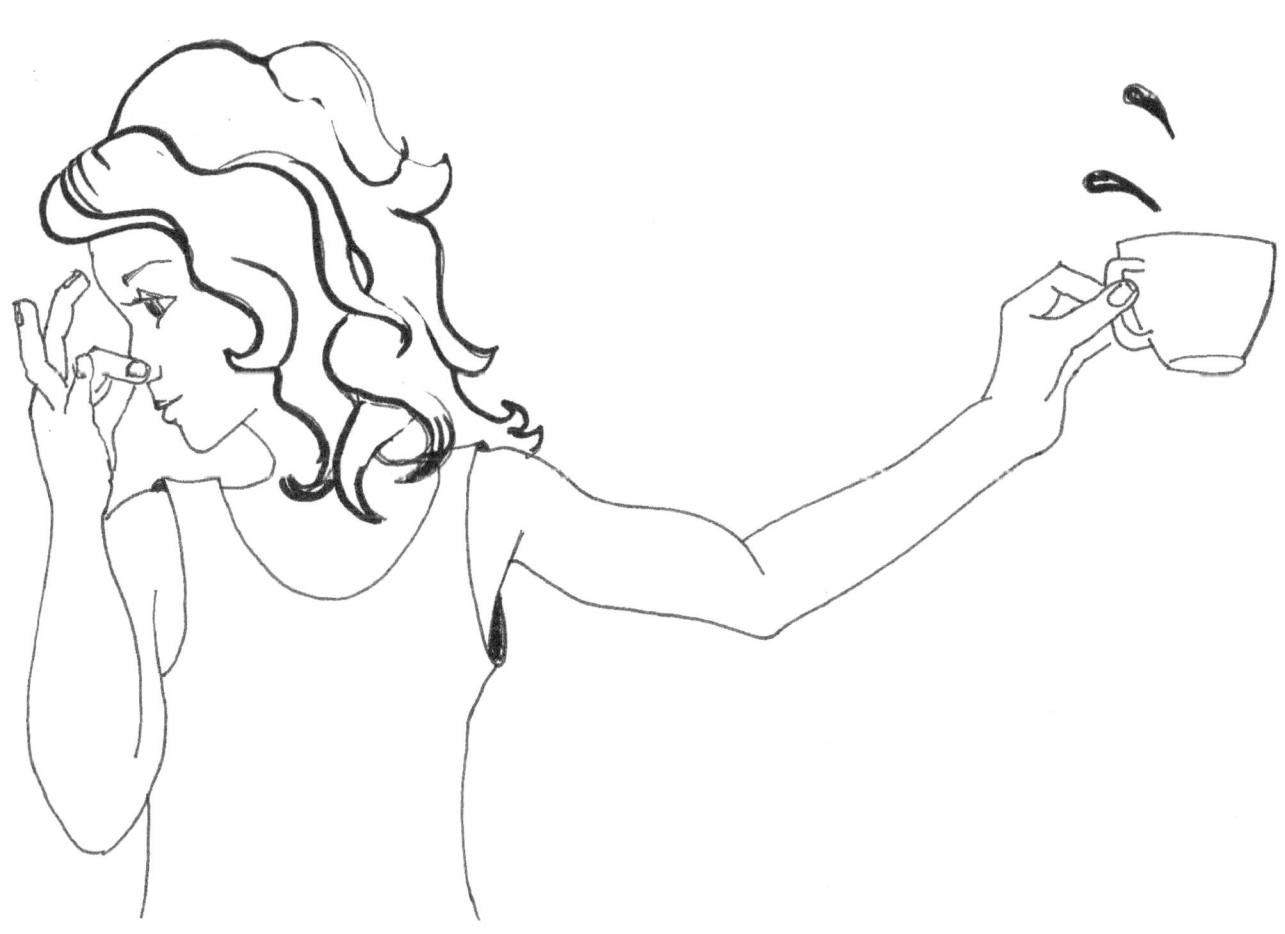

PROTECT OUR WATER

SIGNED:_____

PROTECT OUR WATER

SIGNED:_____

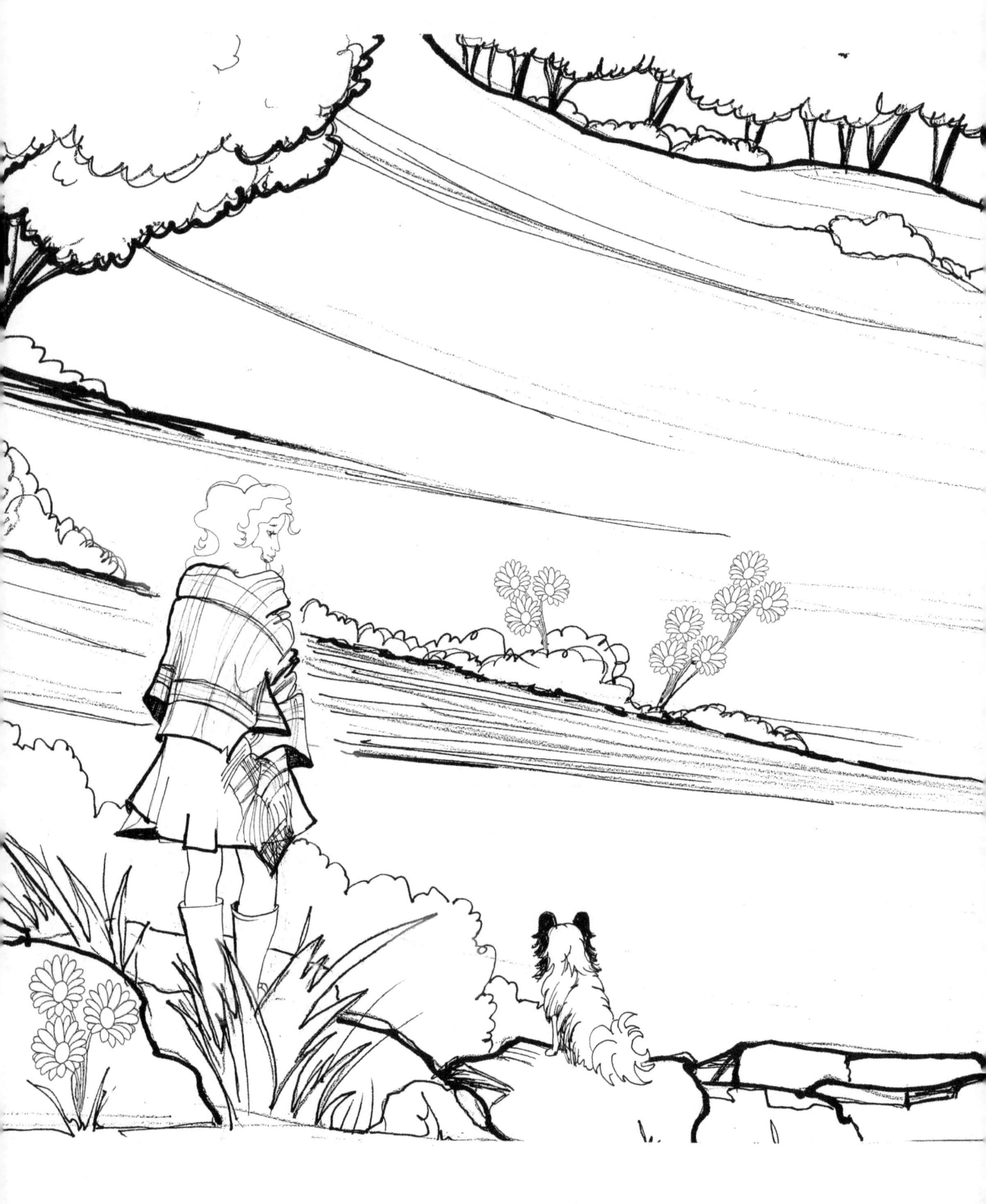

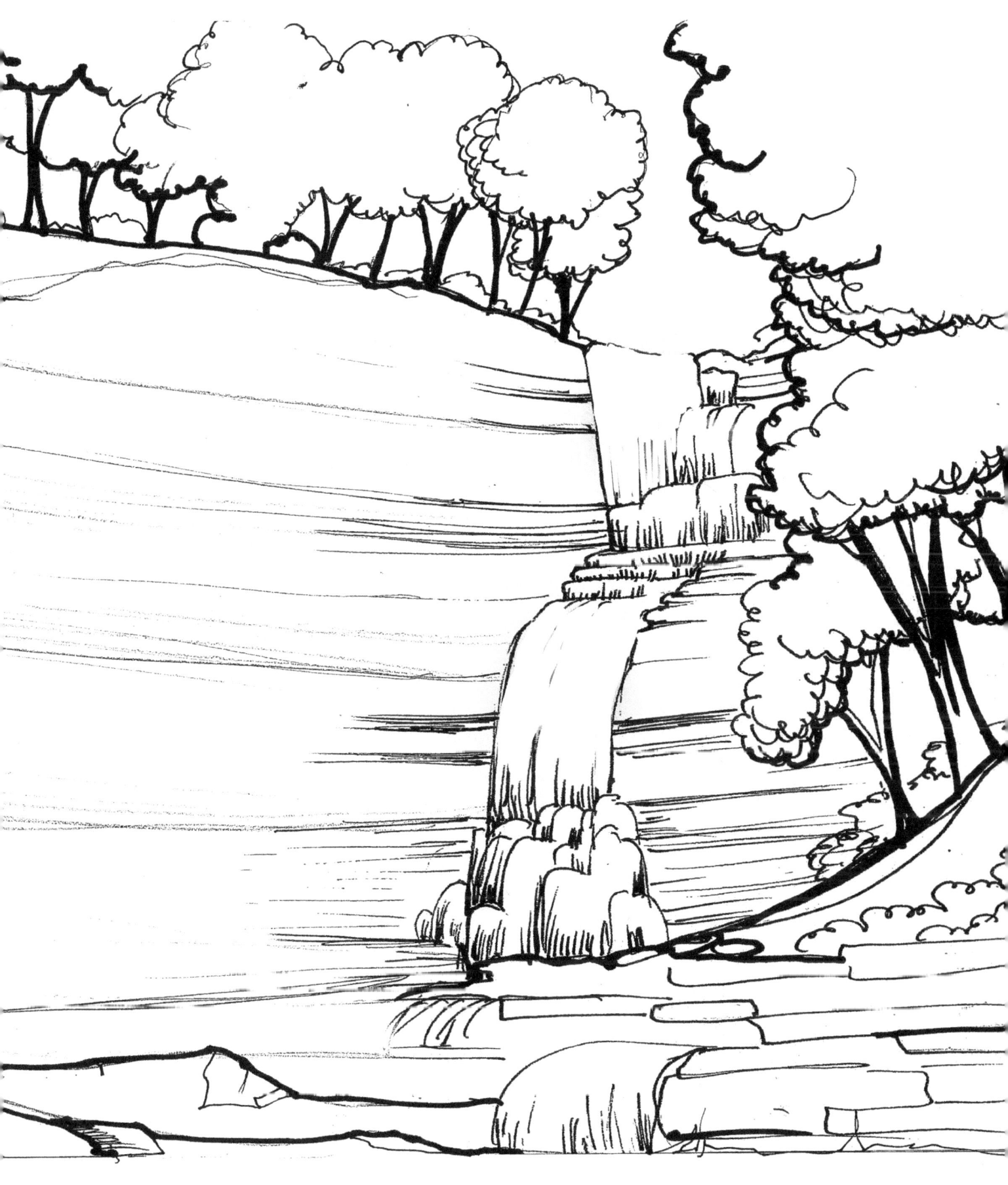

PROTECT OUR WATER

SIGNED:_____

PROTECT OUR WATER

SIGNED:_____

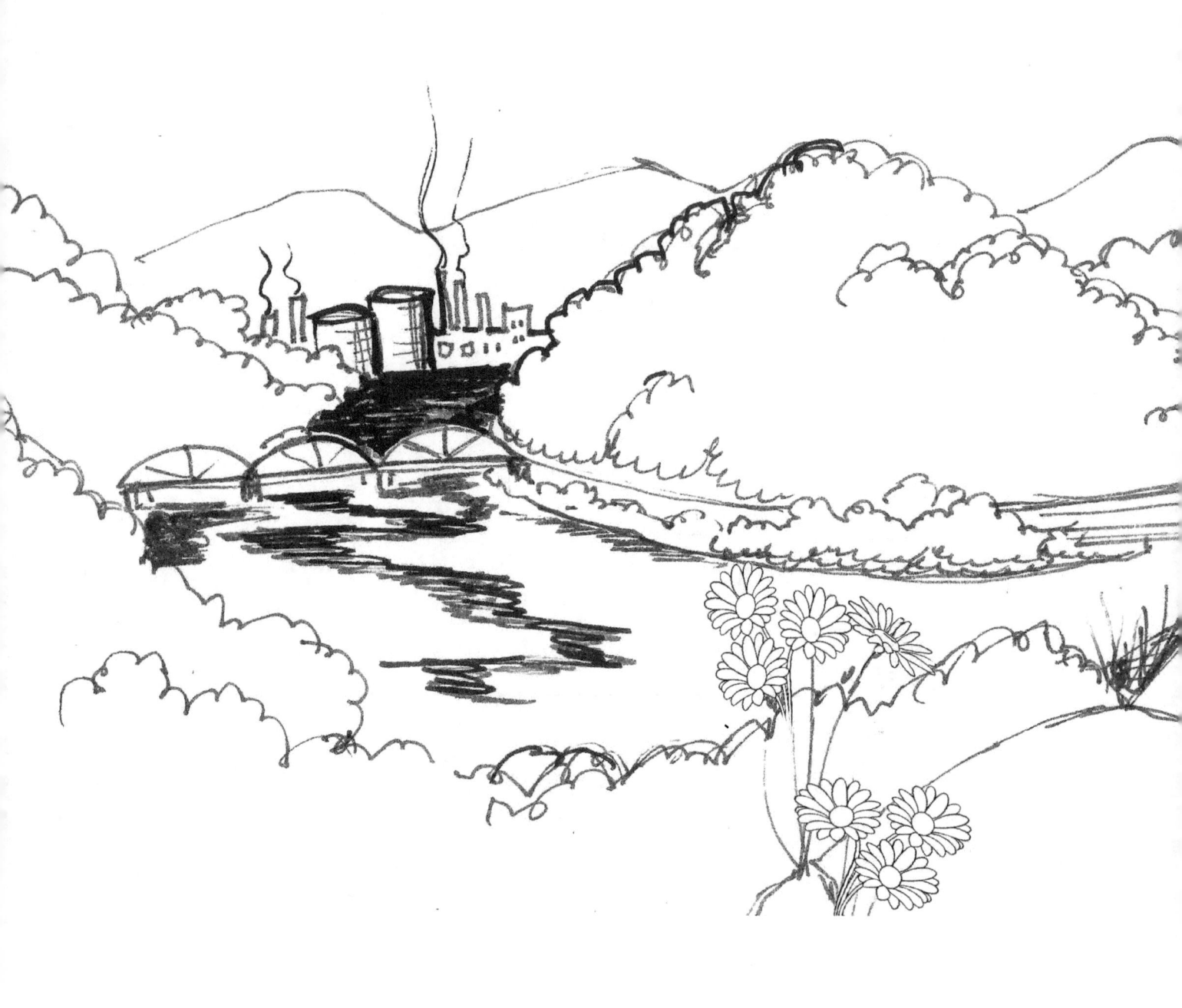

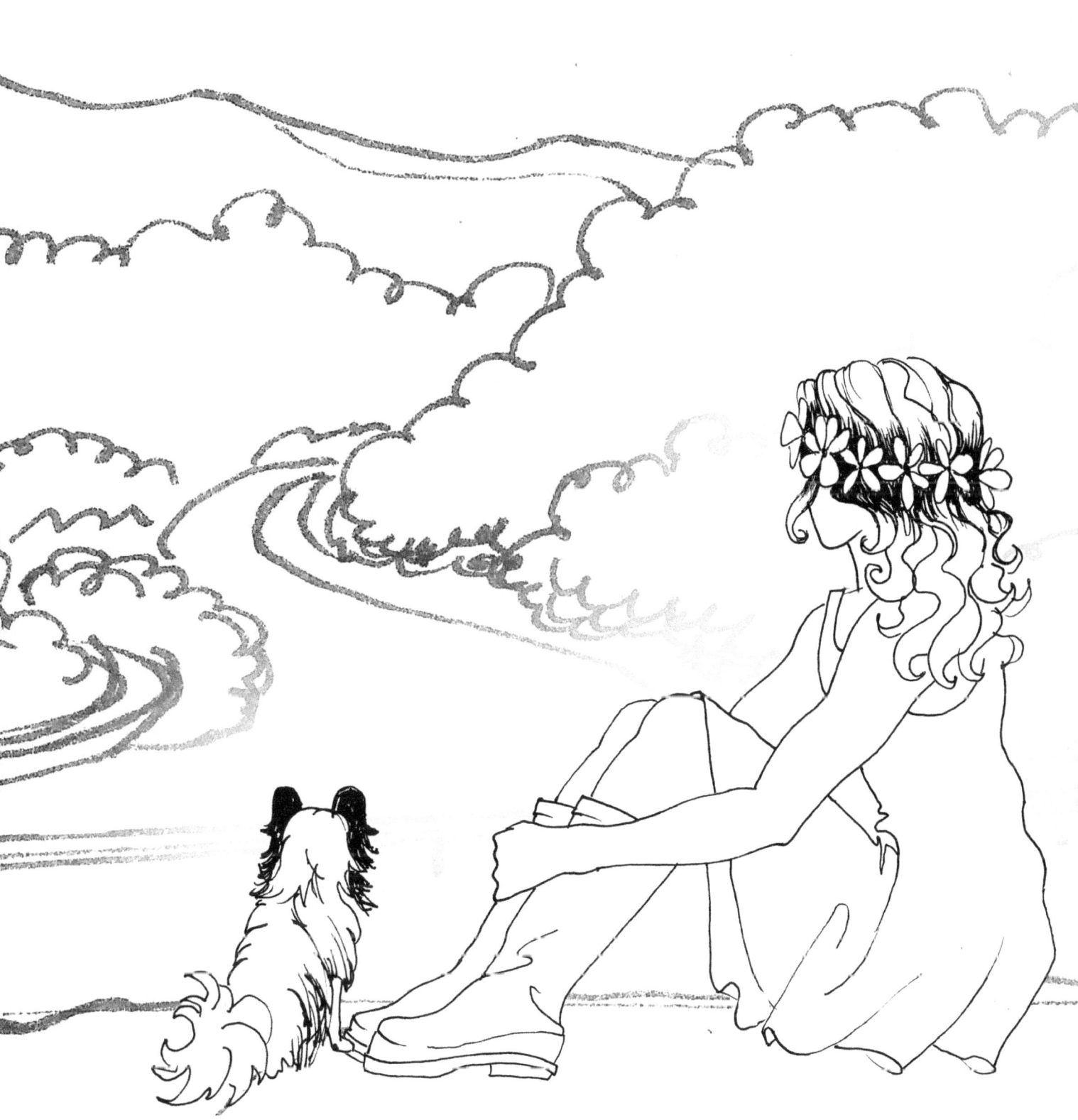

PROTECT OUR
WATER

SIGNED:_____

PROTECT OUR WATER

SIGNED:_____

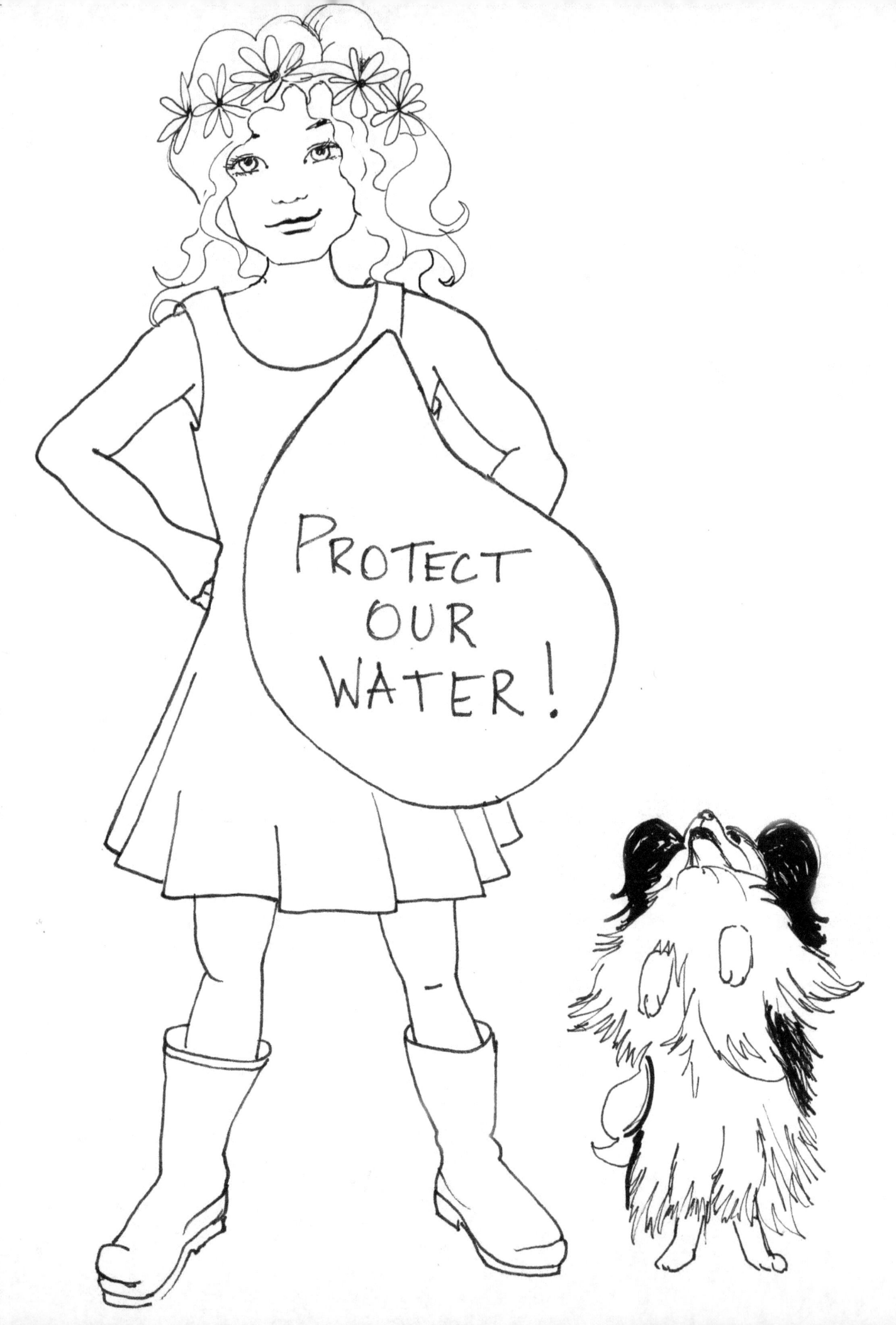

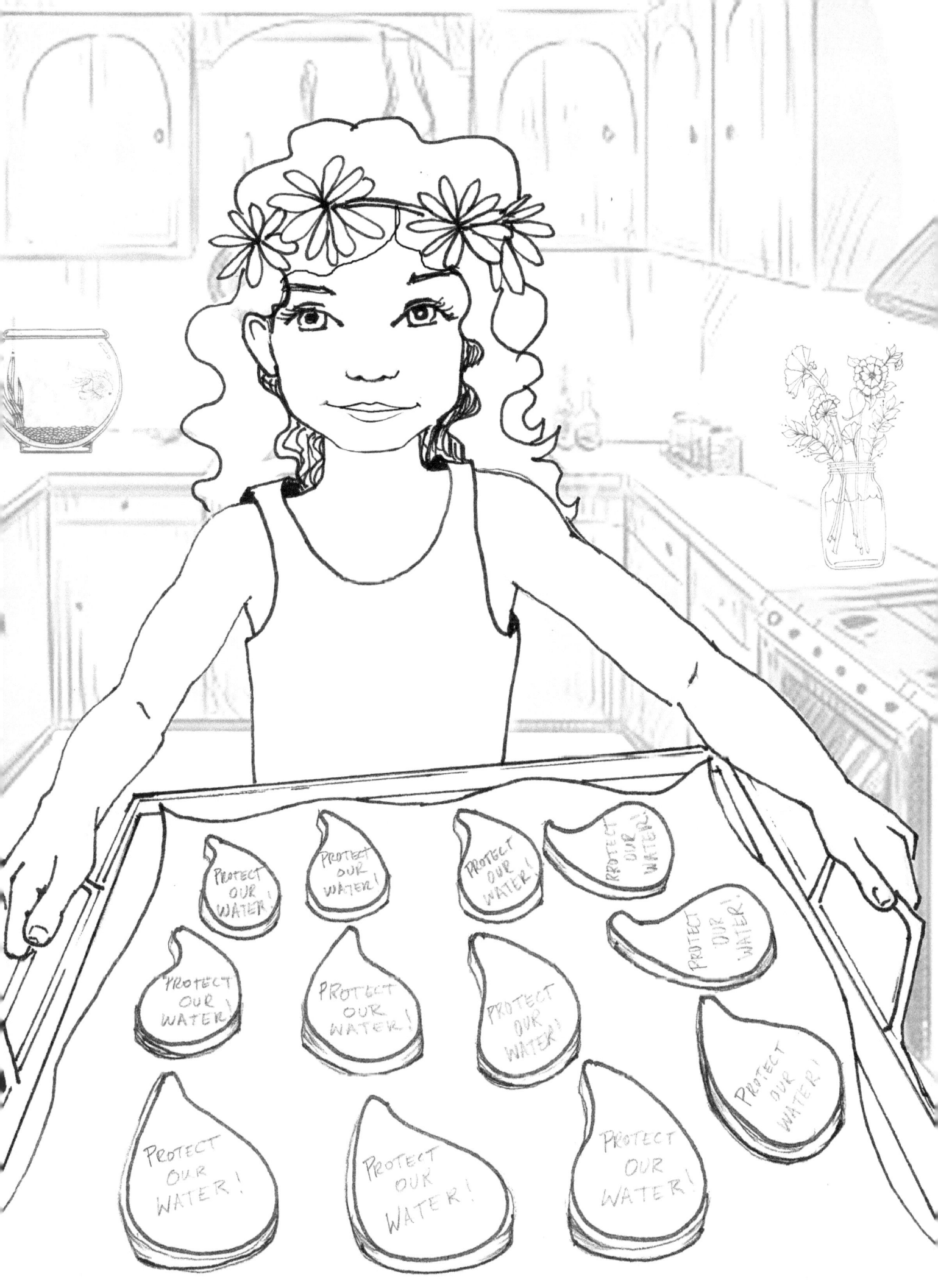

PROTECT OUR WATER

SIGNED:_____

PROTECT OUR WATER

SIGNED:_____

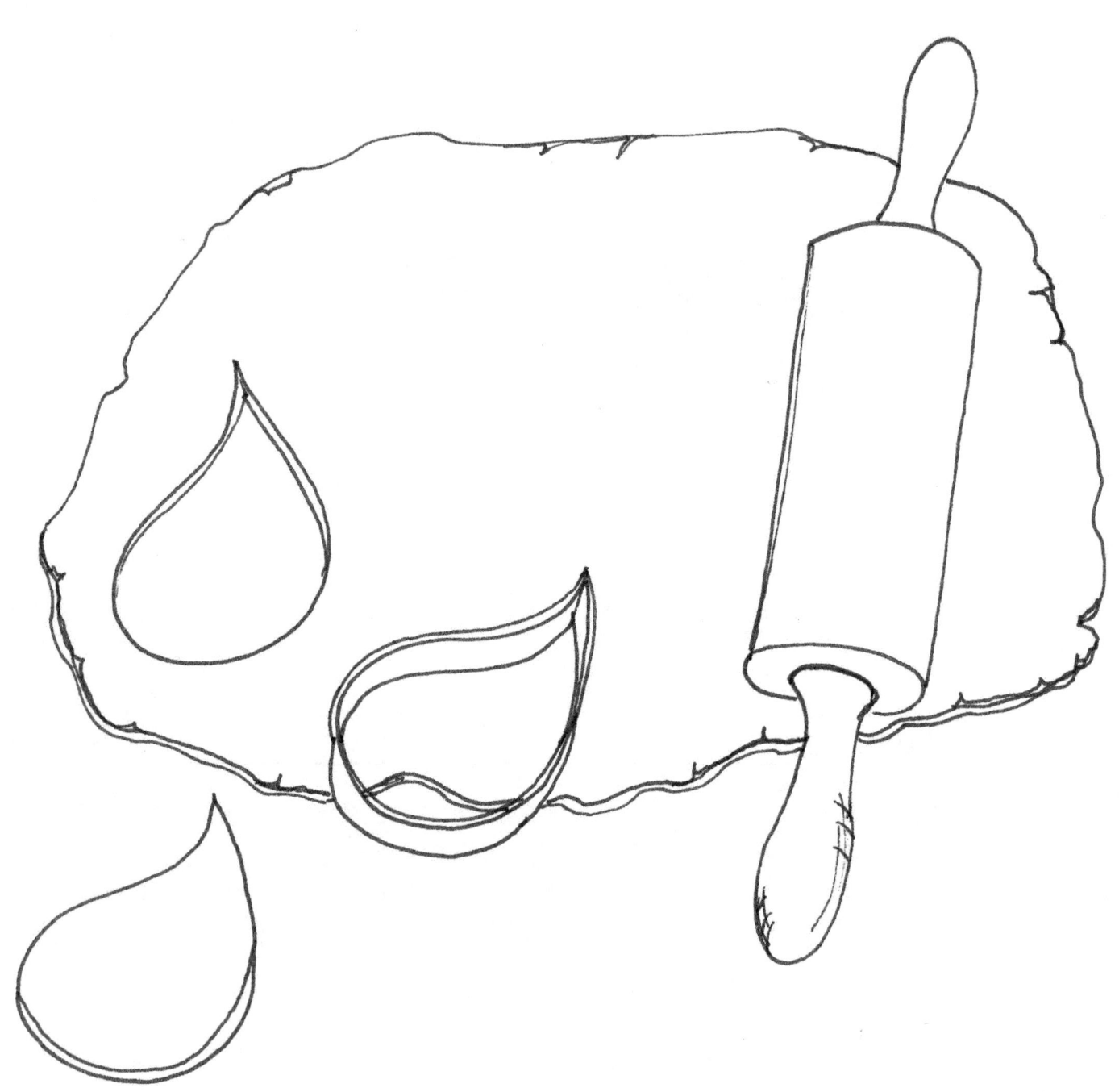

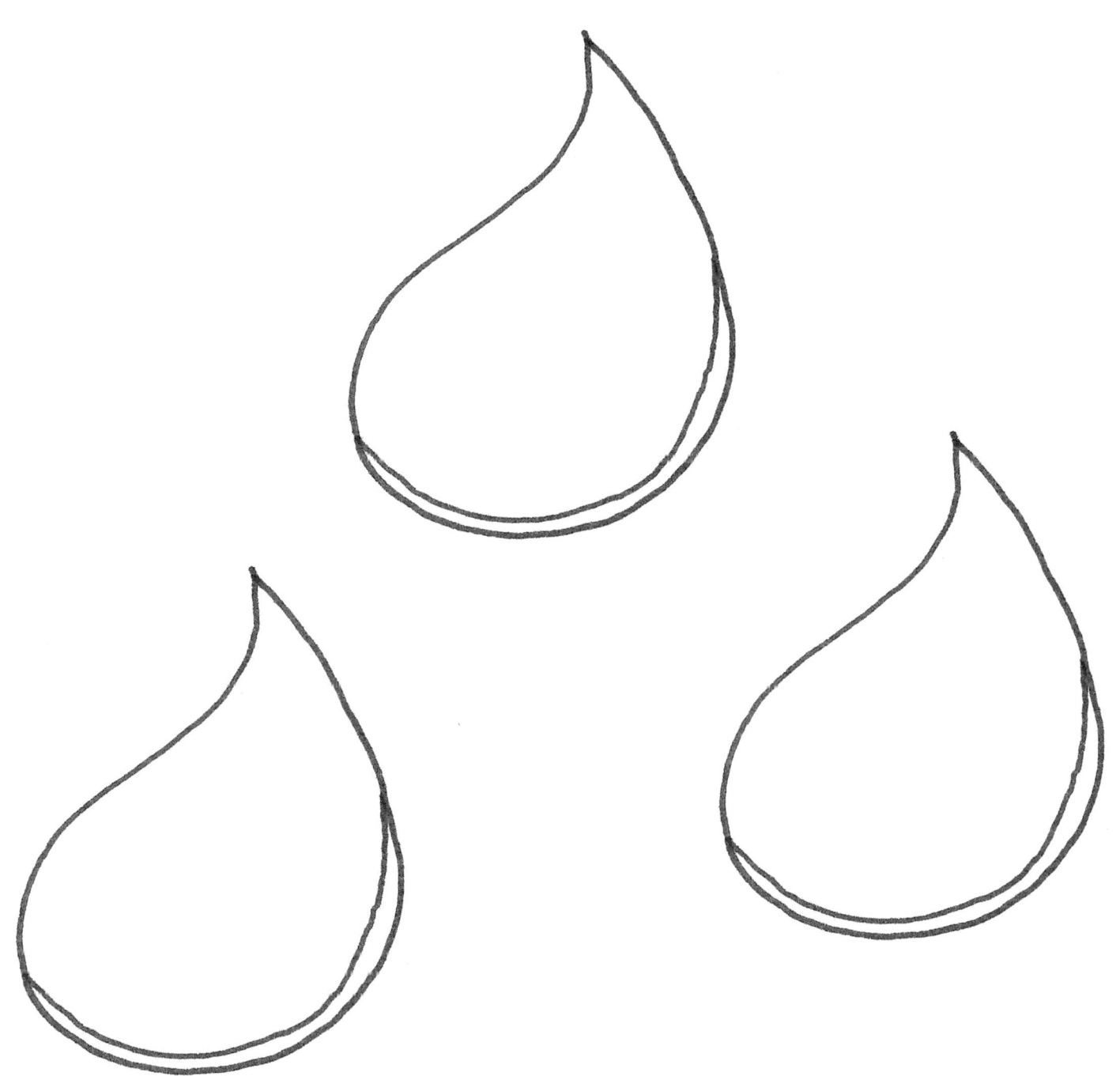

PROTECT OUR WATER

SIGNED:_____

PROTECT OUR WATER

SIGNED:_____

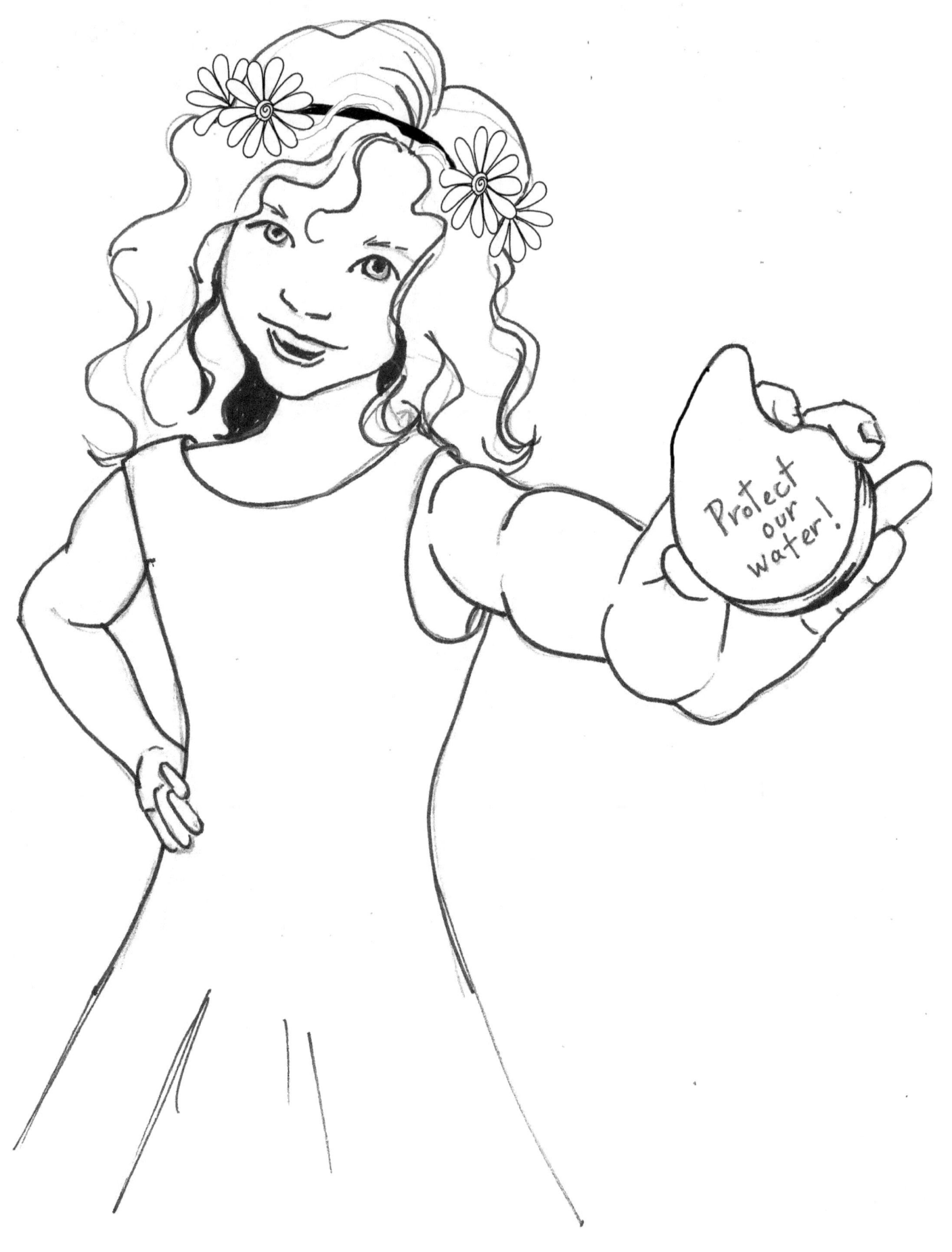

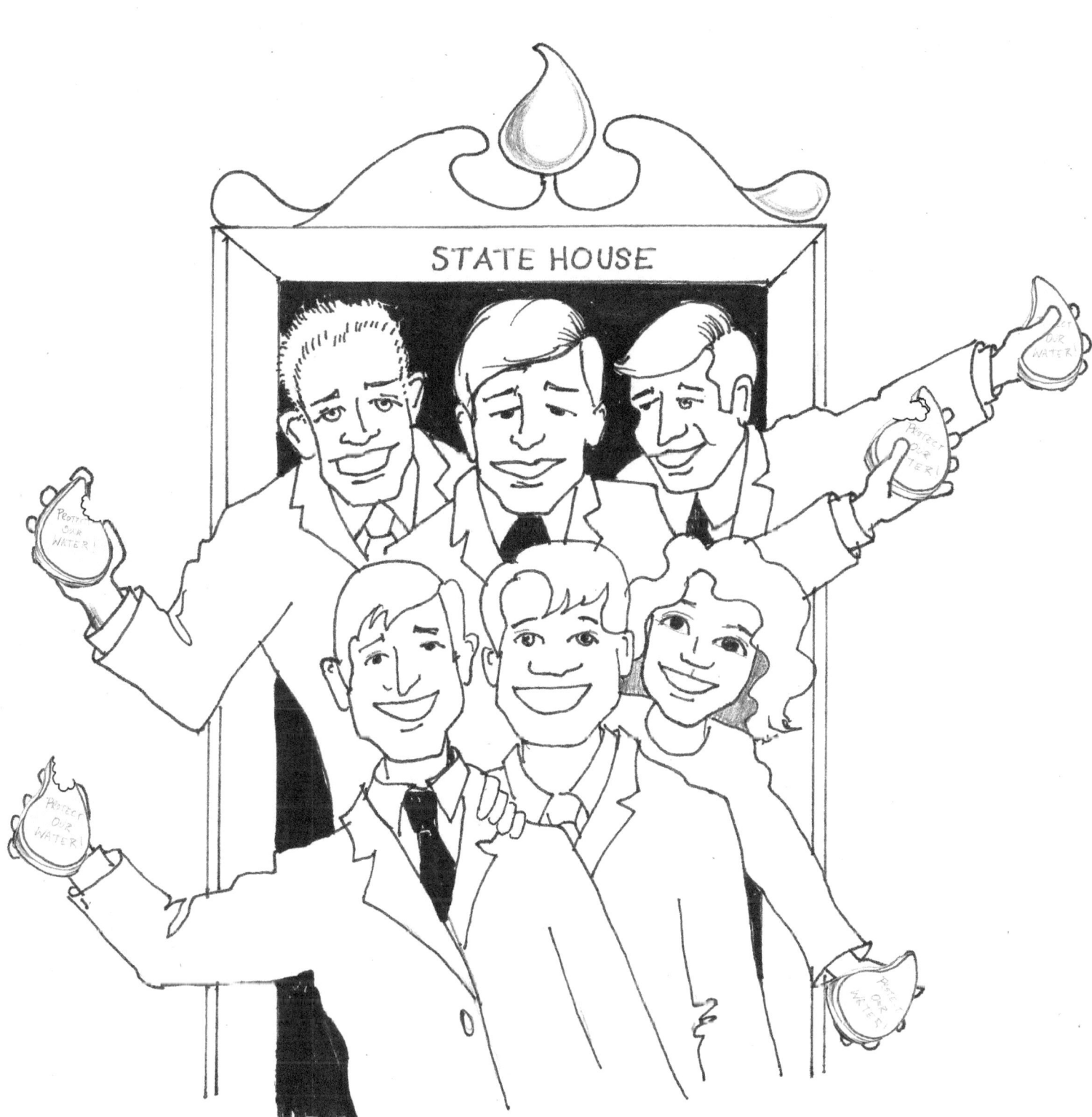

PROTECT OUR WATER

SIGNED:_____

PROTECT OUR WATER

SIGNED:_____

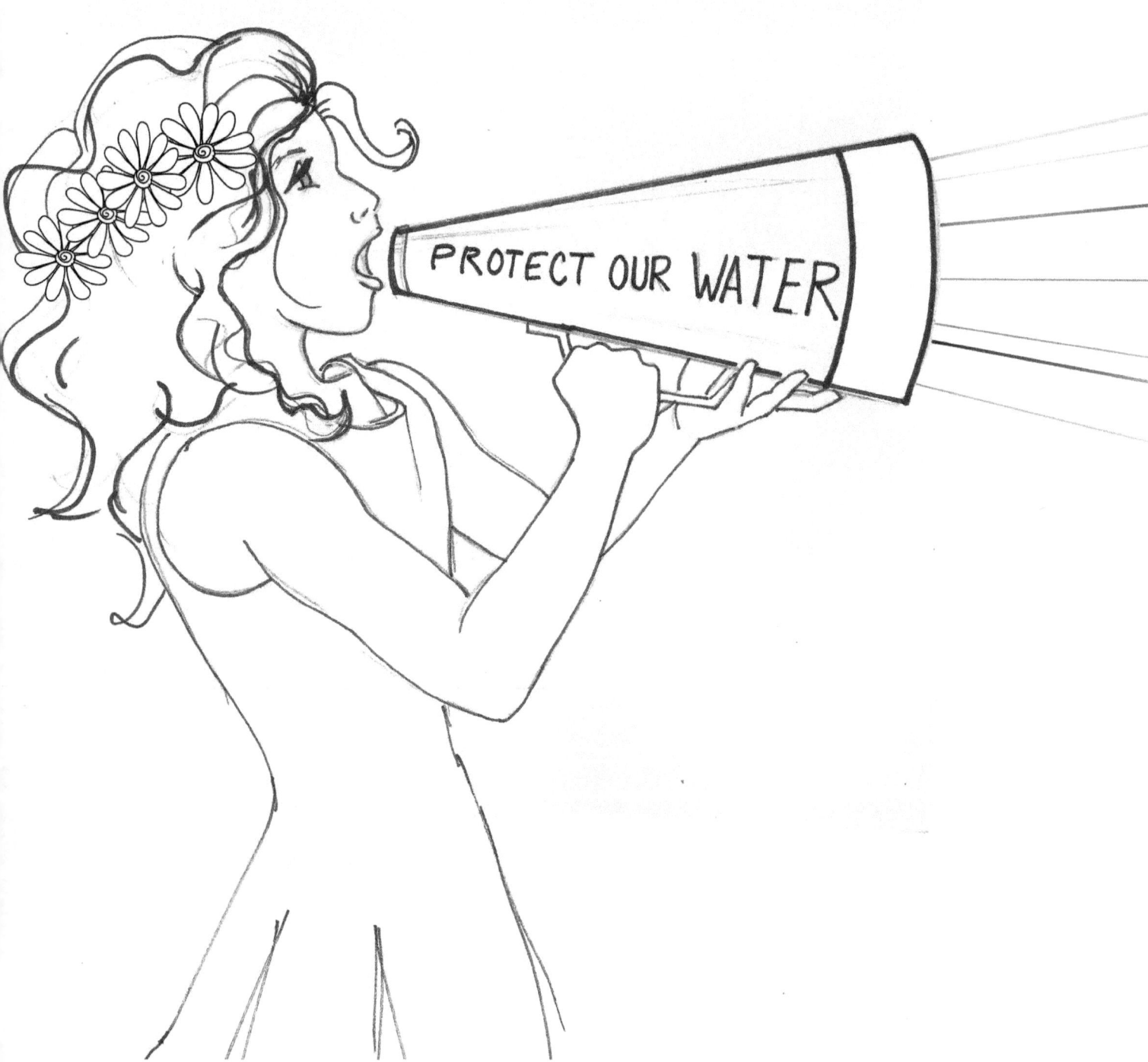

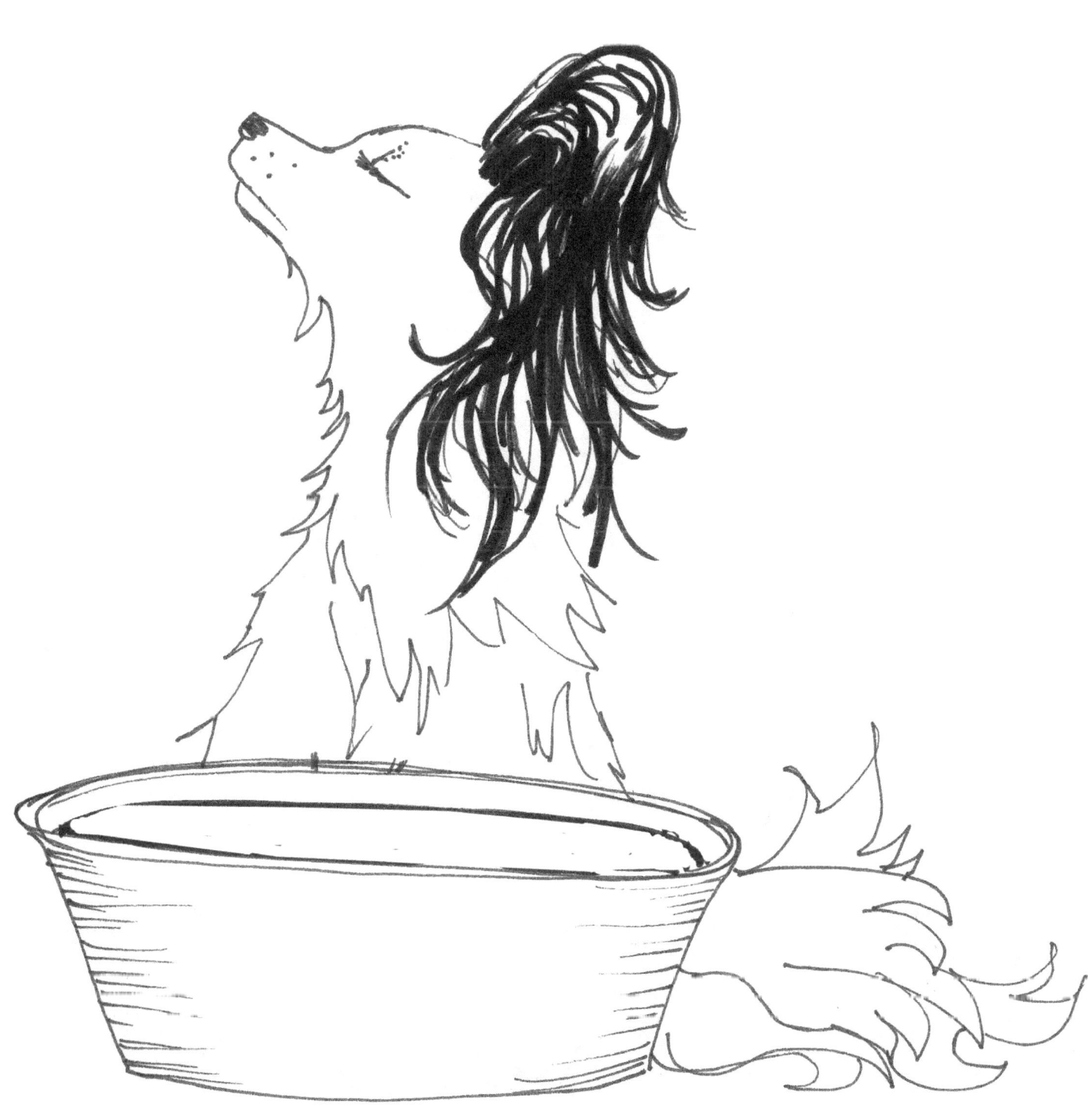

PROTECT OUR WATER

SIGNED:_____

PROTECT OUR WATER

SIGNED:_____

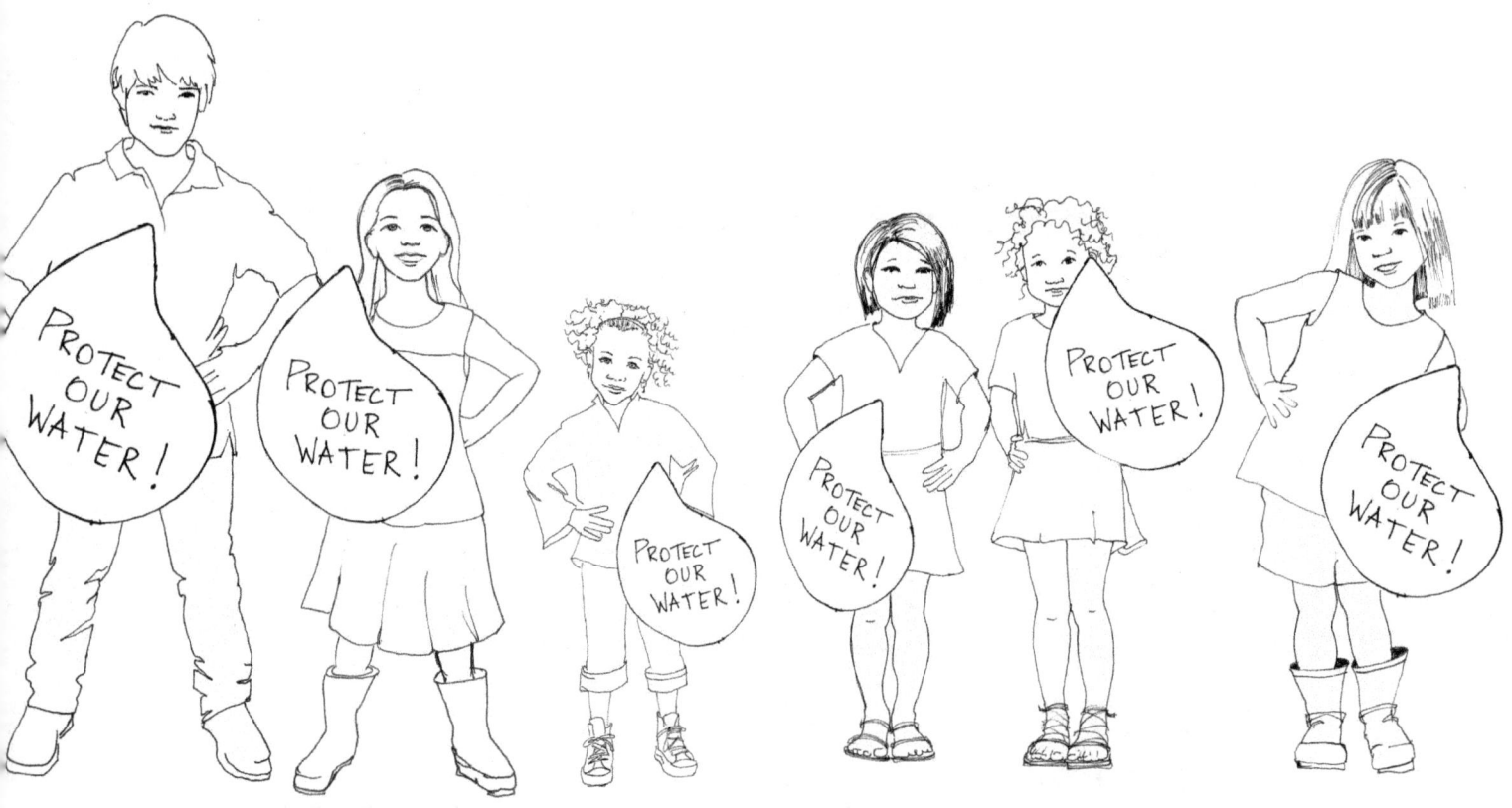

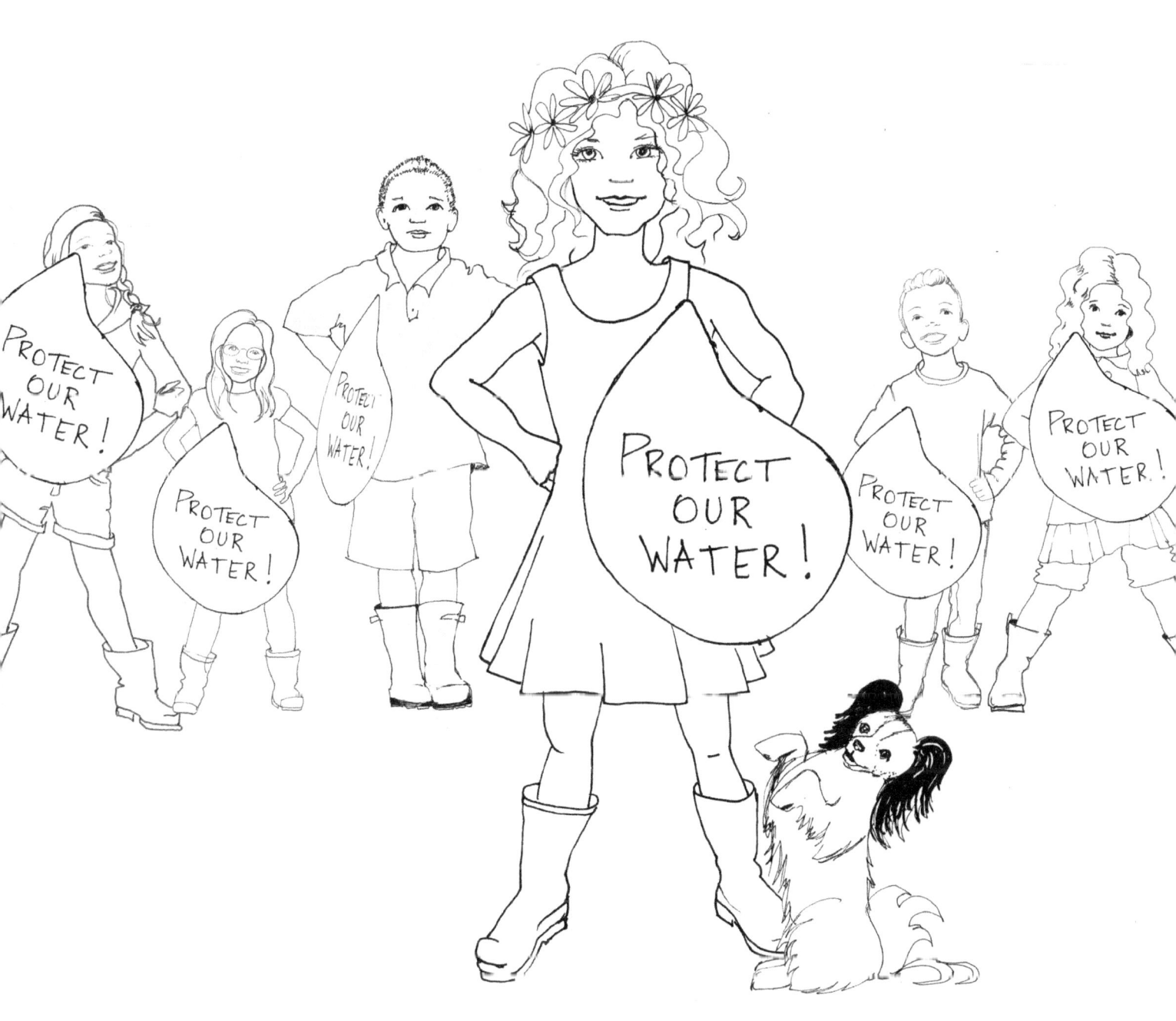

PROTECT OUR WATER

SIGNED:_____

PROTECT OUR WATER

SIGNED:_____

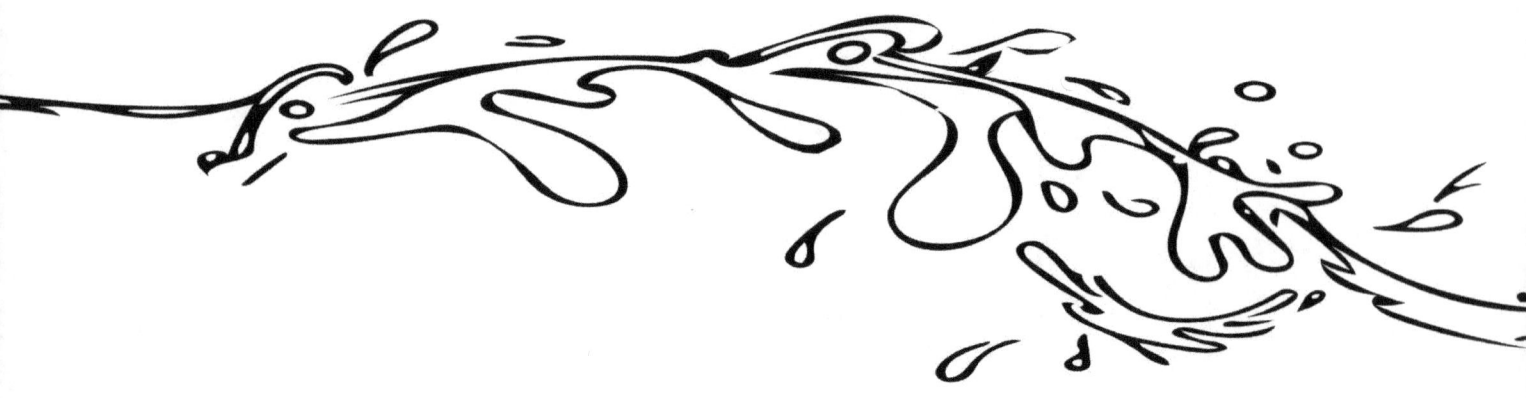

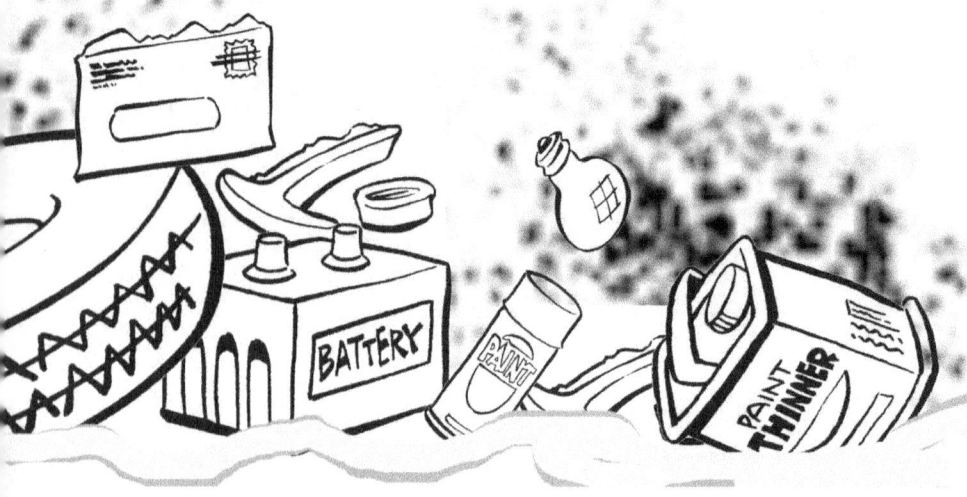

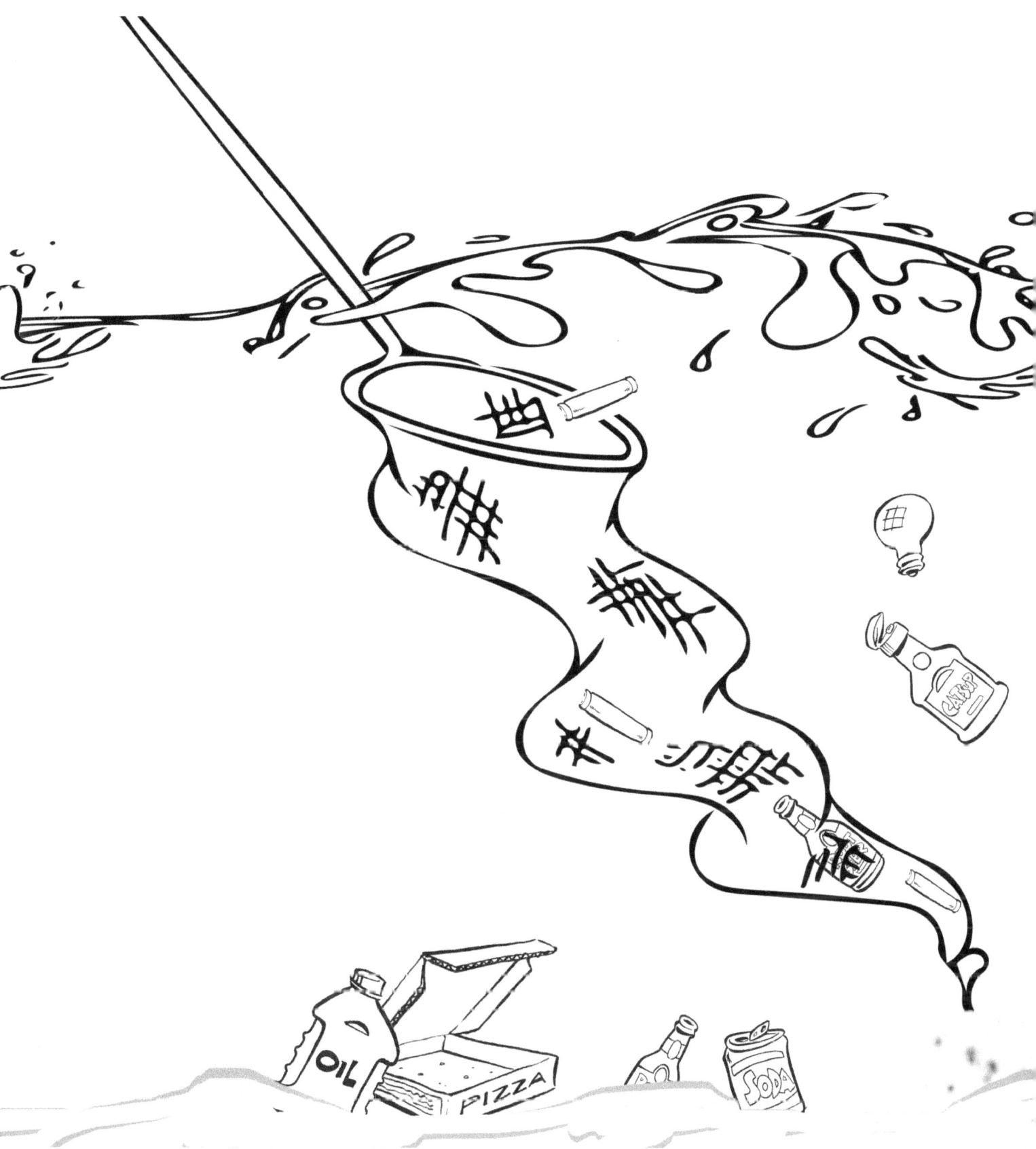

PROTECT OUR
WATER

SIGNED:_____

PROTECT OUR
WATER

SIGNED:_____

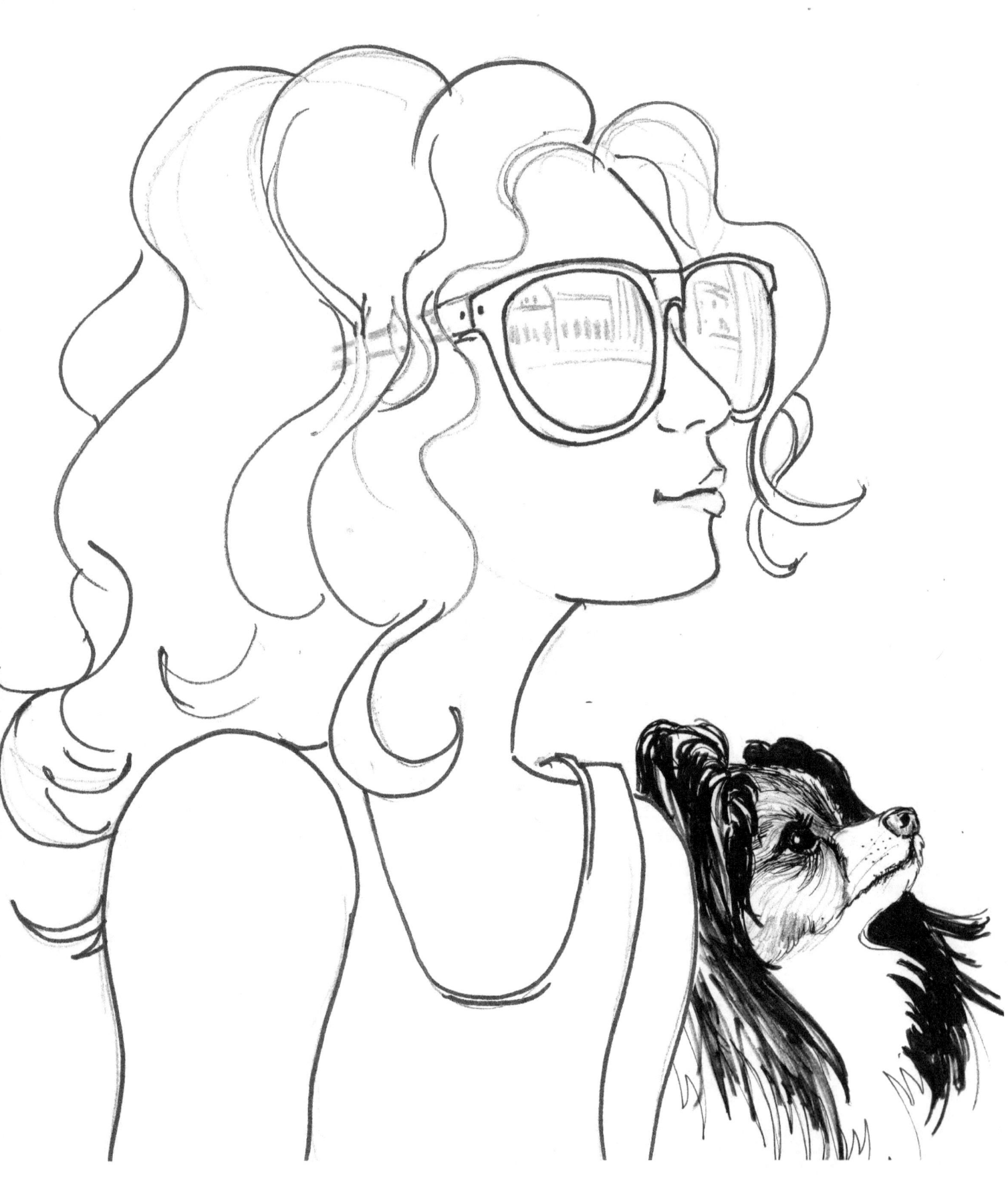

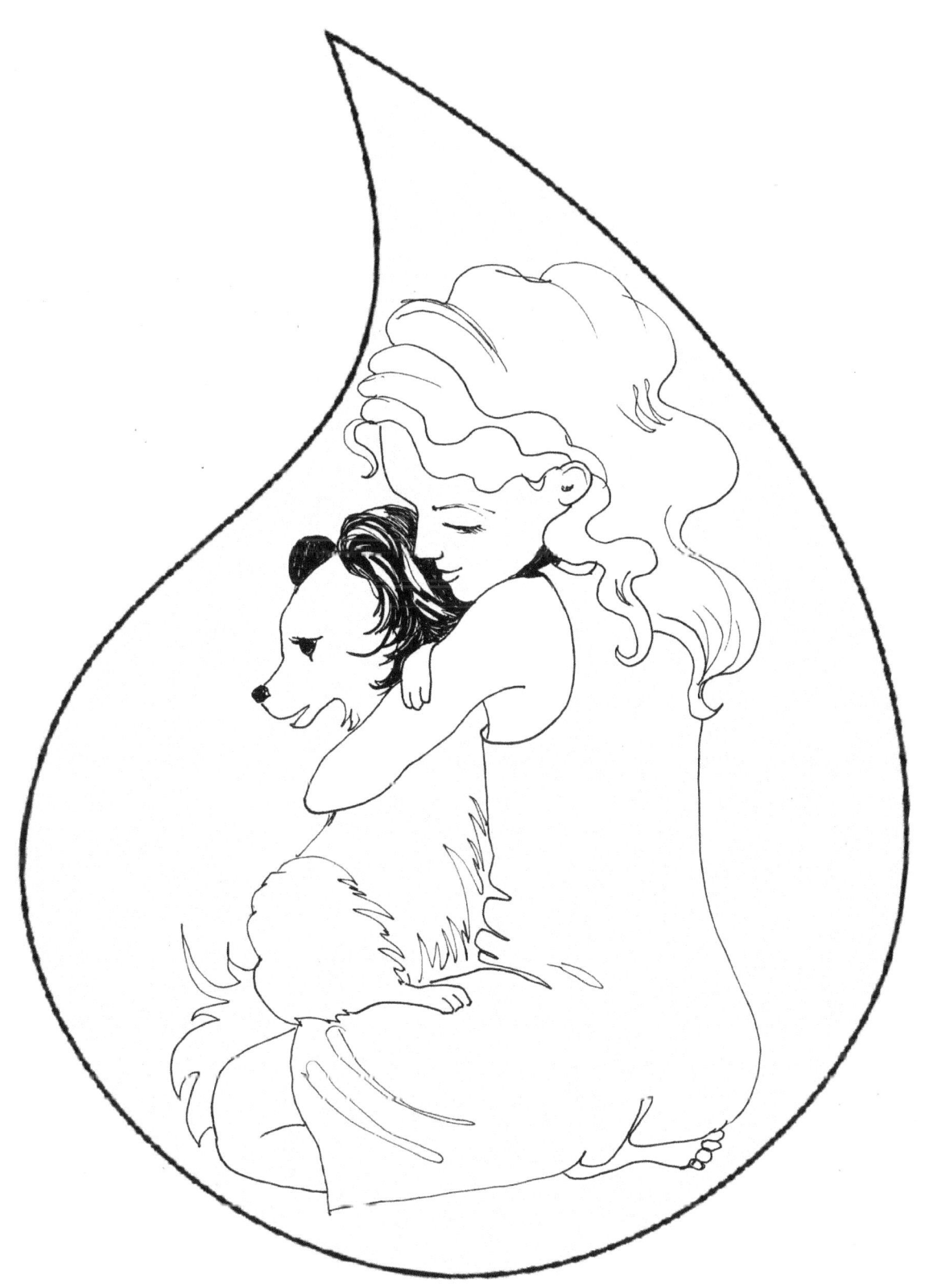

PROTECT OUR WATER

SIGNED:_____

PROTECT OUR WATER

SIGNED:_____

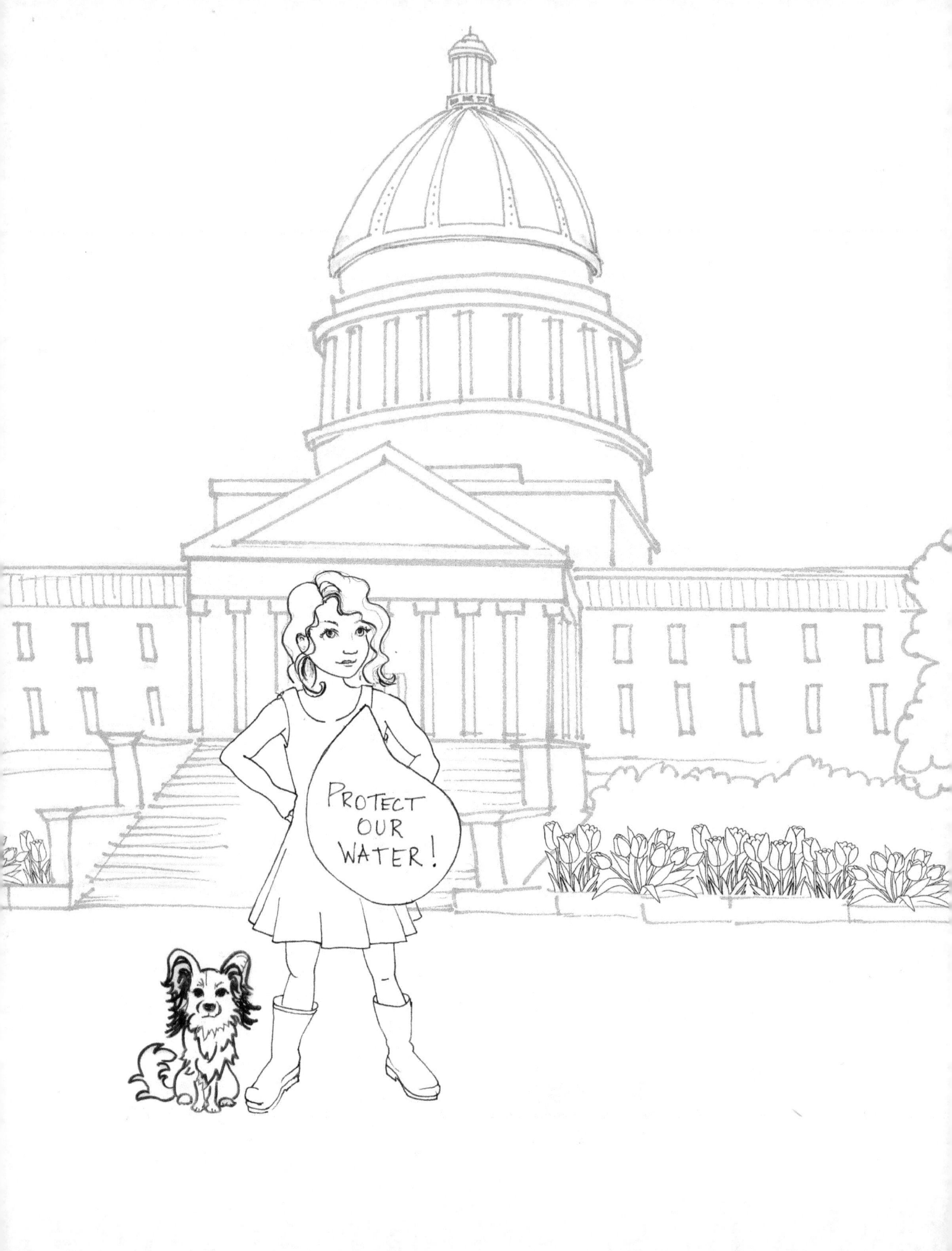

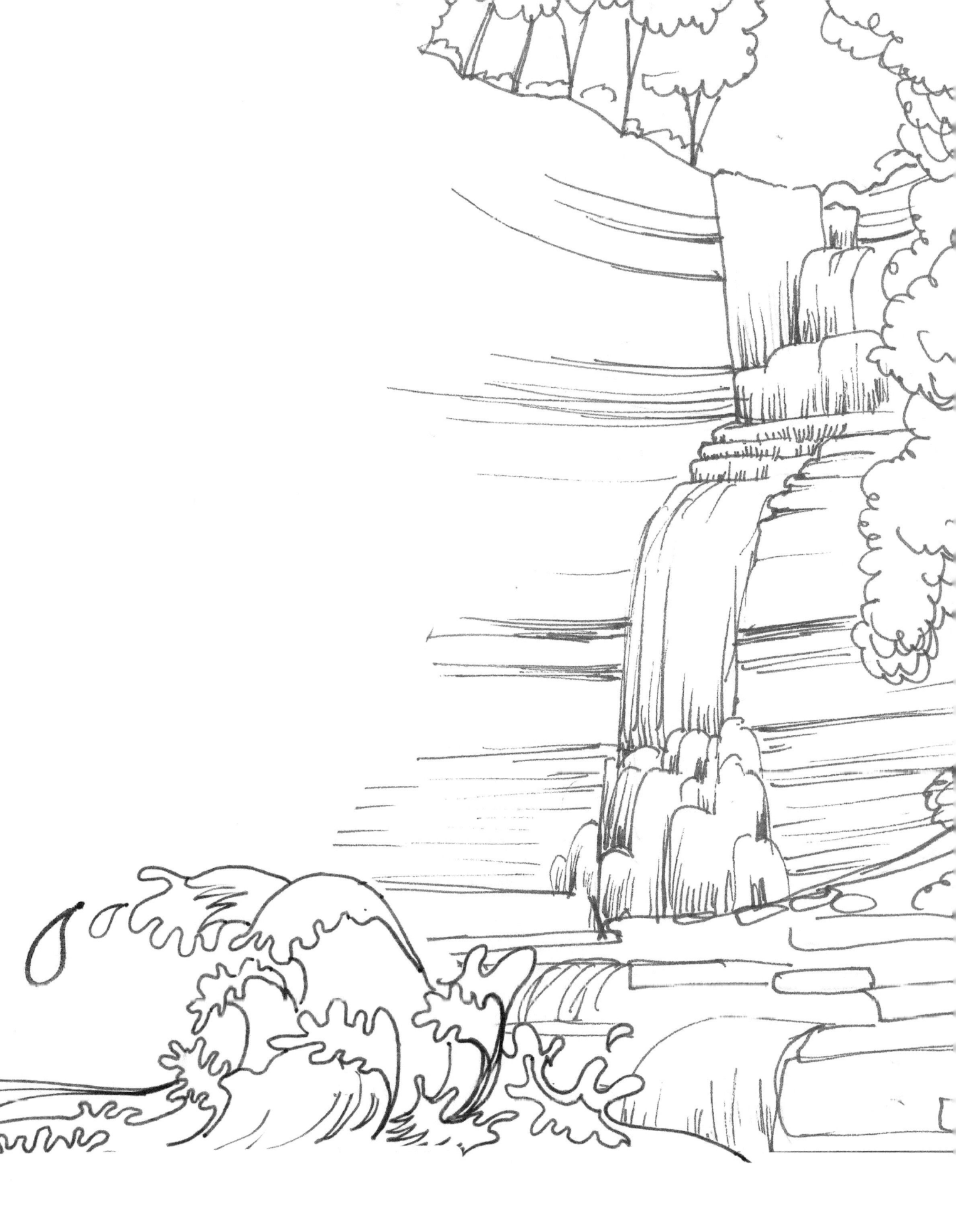

PROTECT OUR WATER

SIGNED:_____

PROTECT OUR WATER

SIGNED:_____

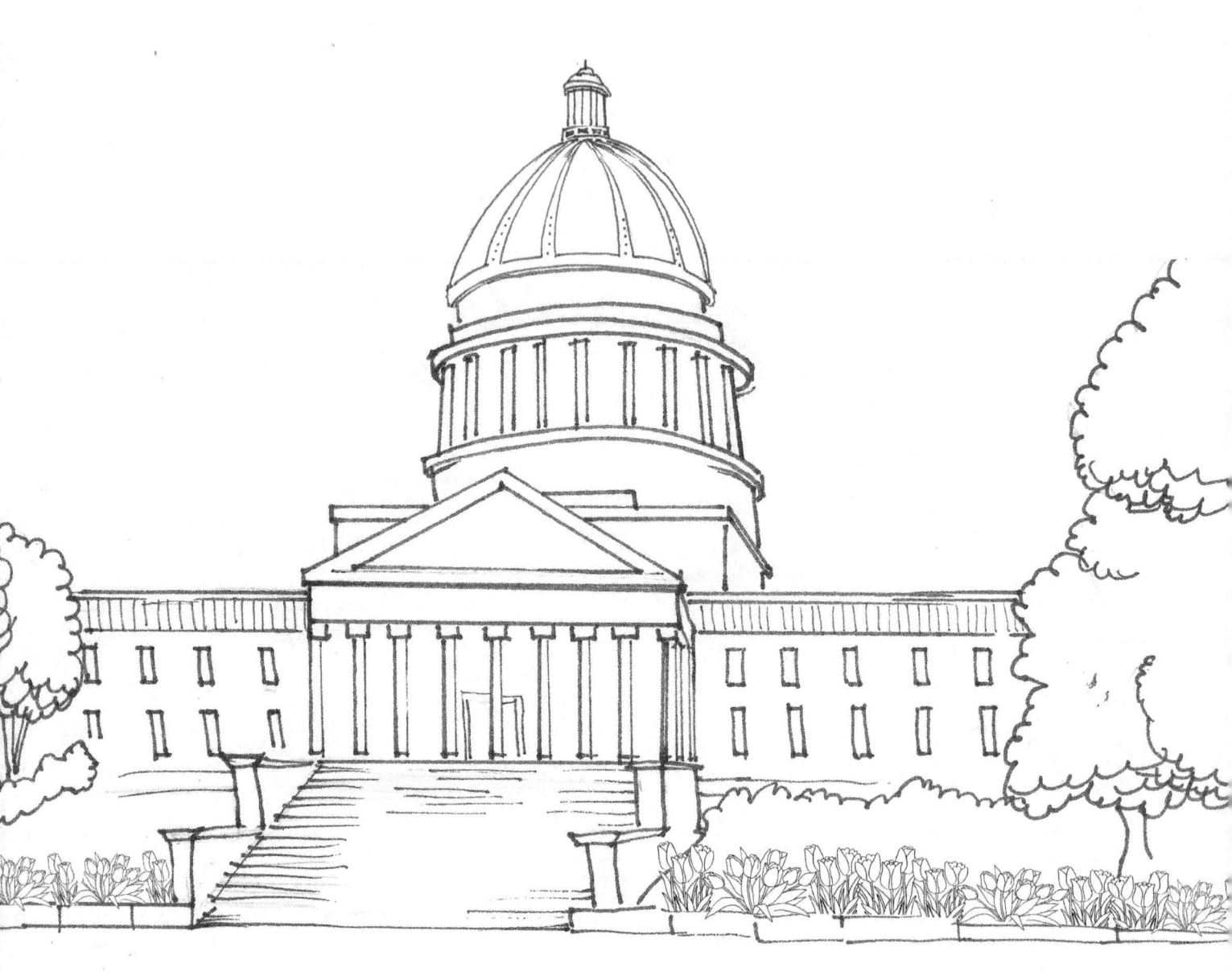

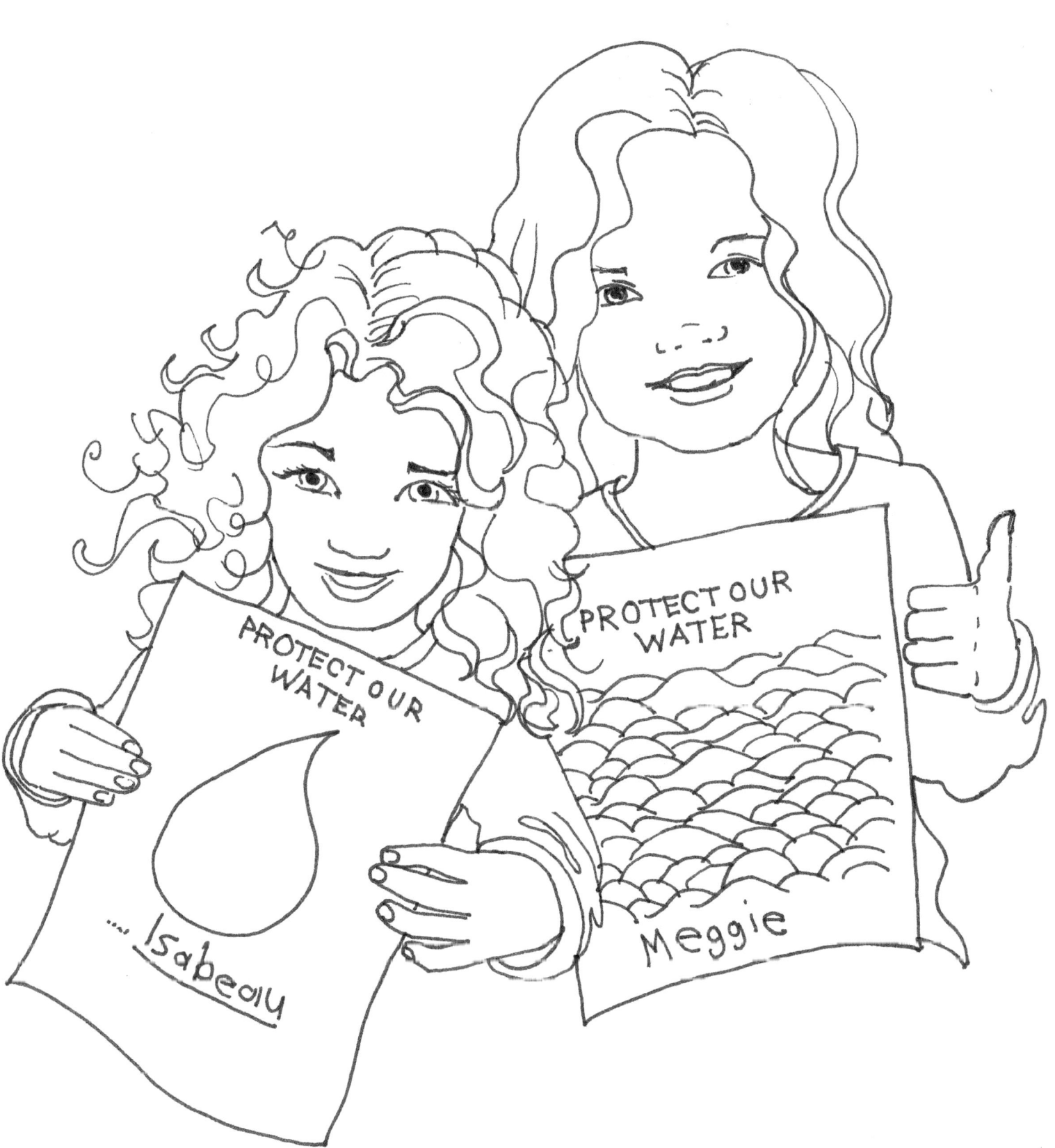

PROTECT OUR WATER

SIGNED:_____

PROTECT OUR
WATER

SIGNED:_____

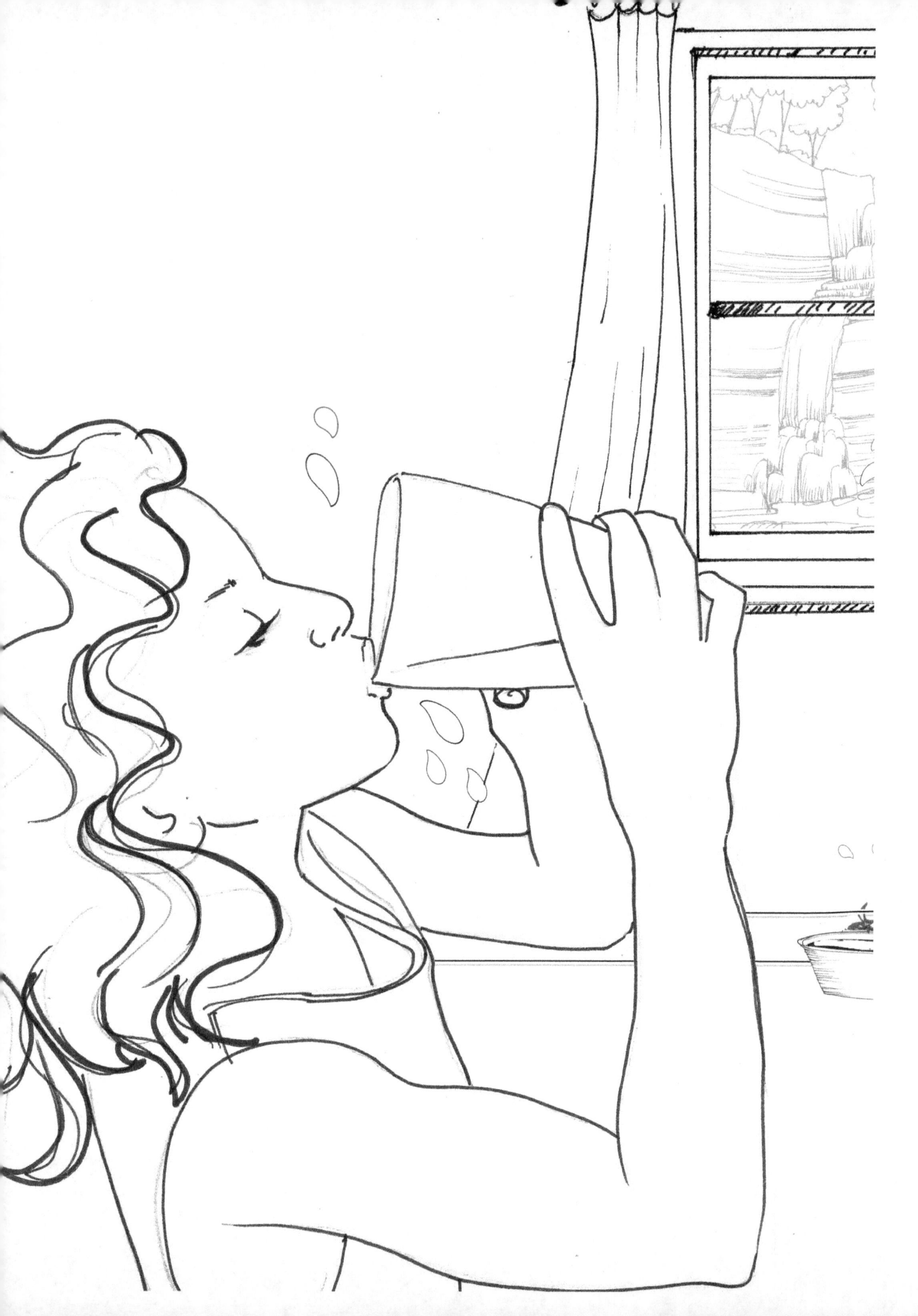

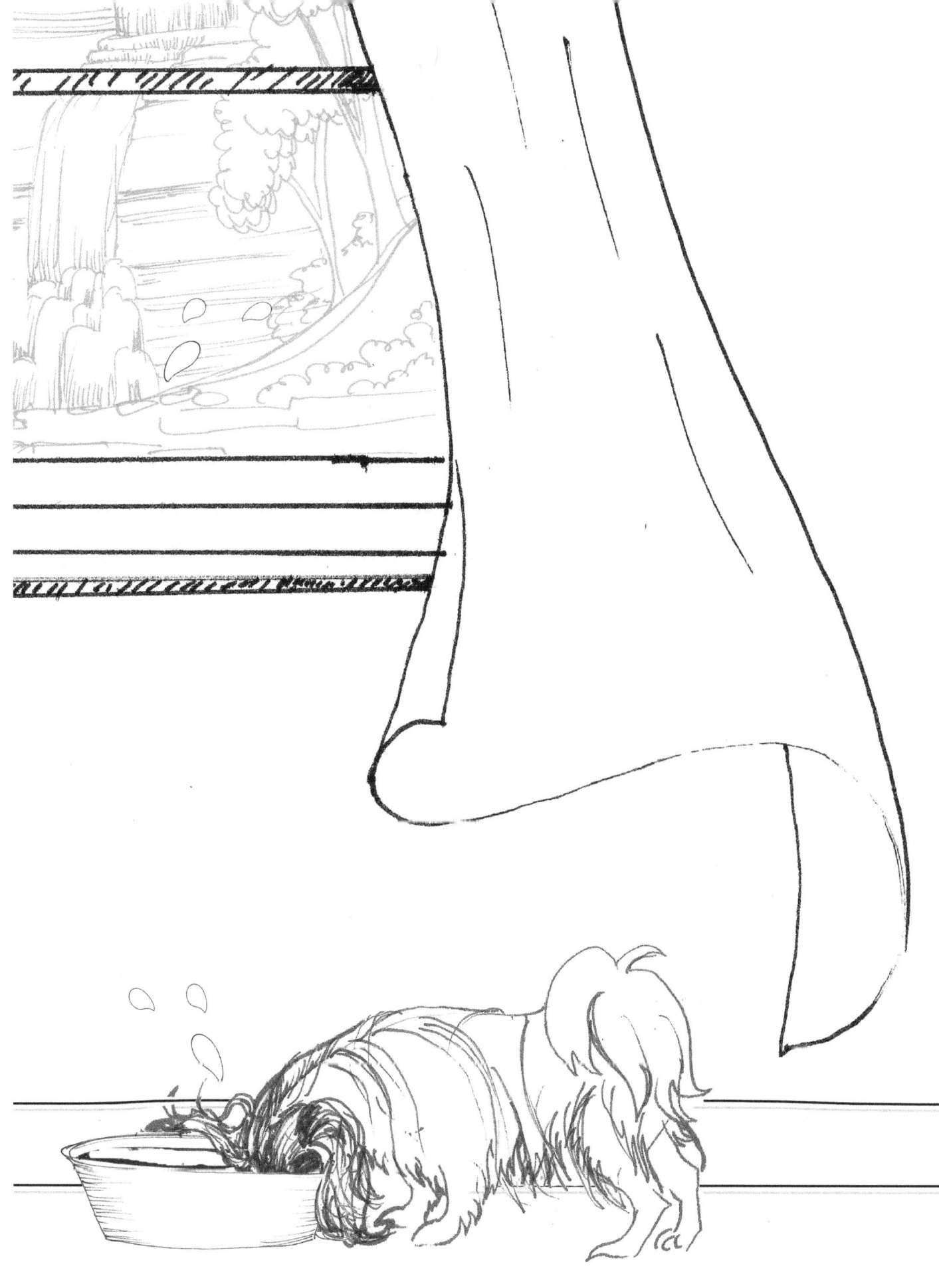

PROTECT OUR WATER

SIGNED:_____

PROTECT OUR
WATER

SIGNED:_____

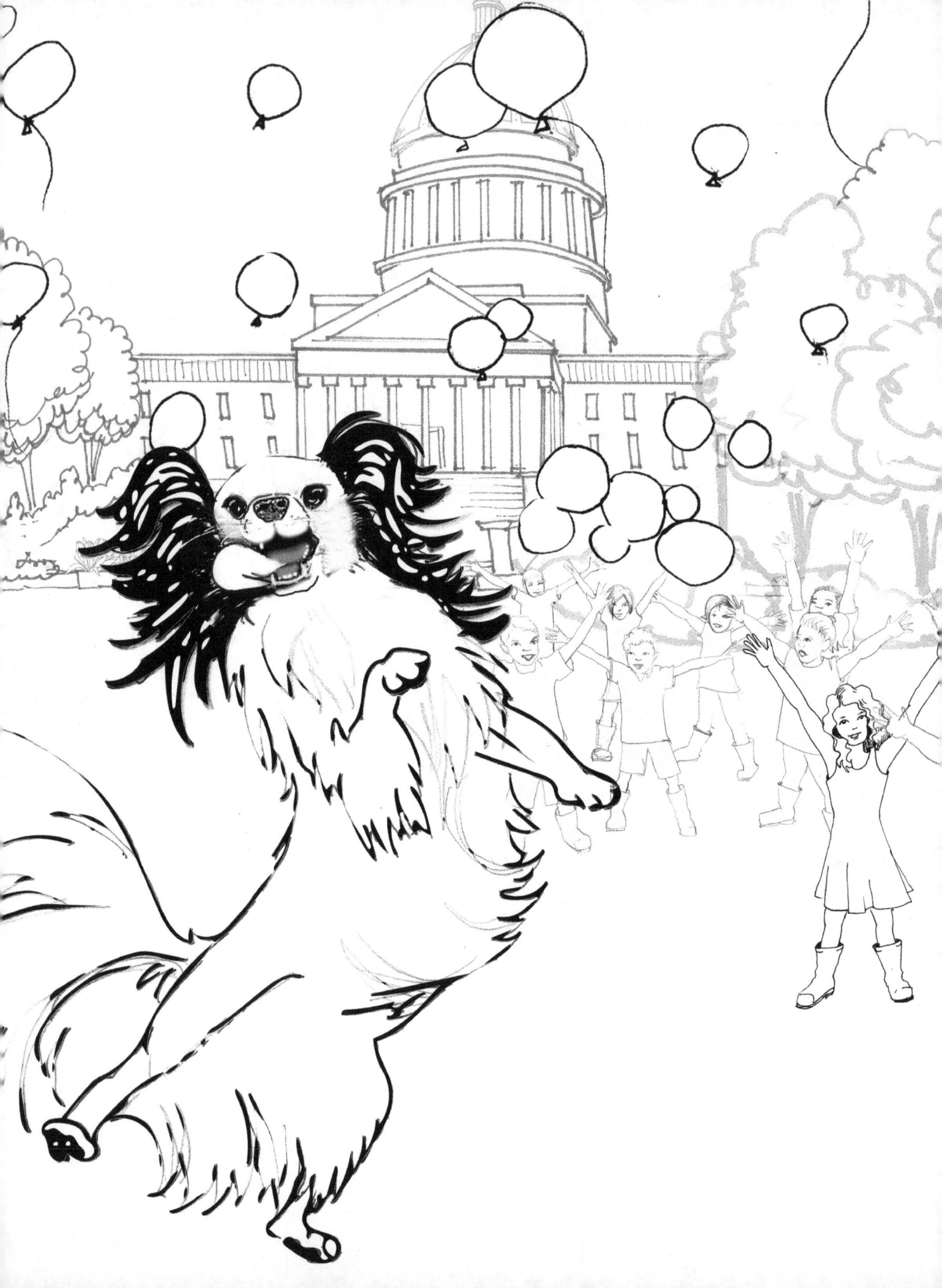

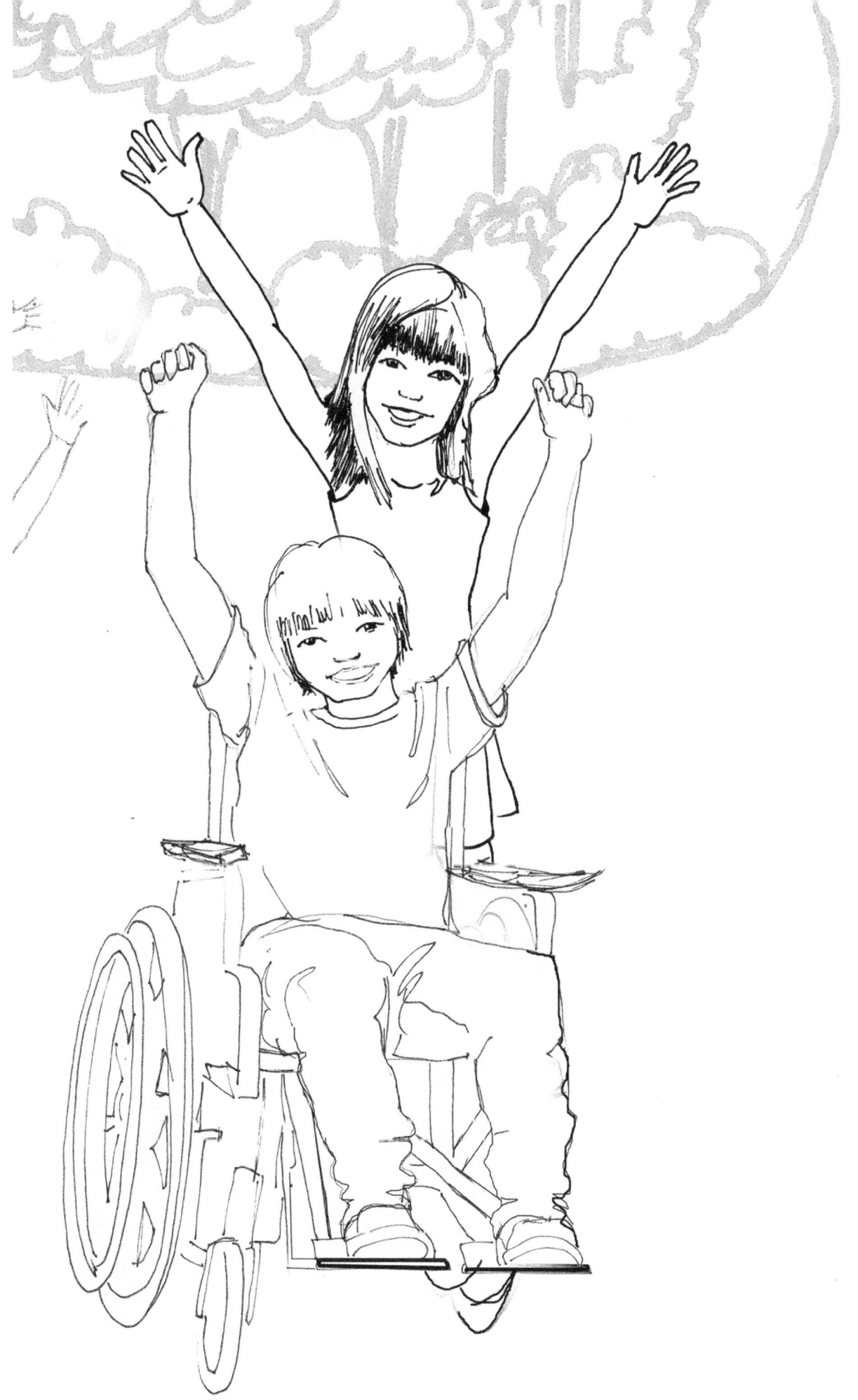

PROTECT OUR WATER

SIGNED:_____

PROTECT OUR WATER

SIGNED:_____

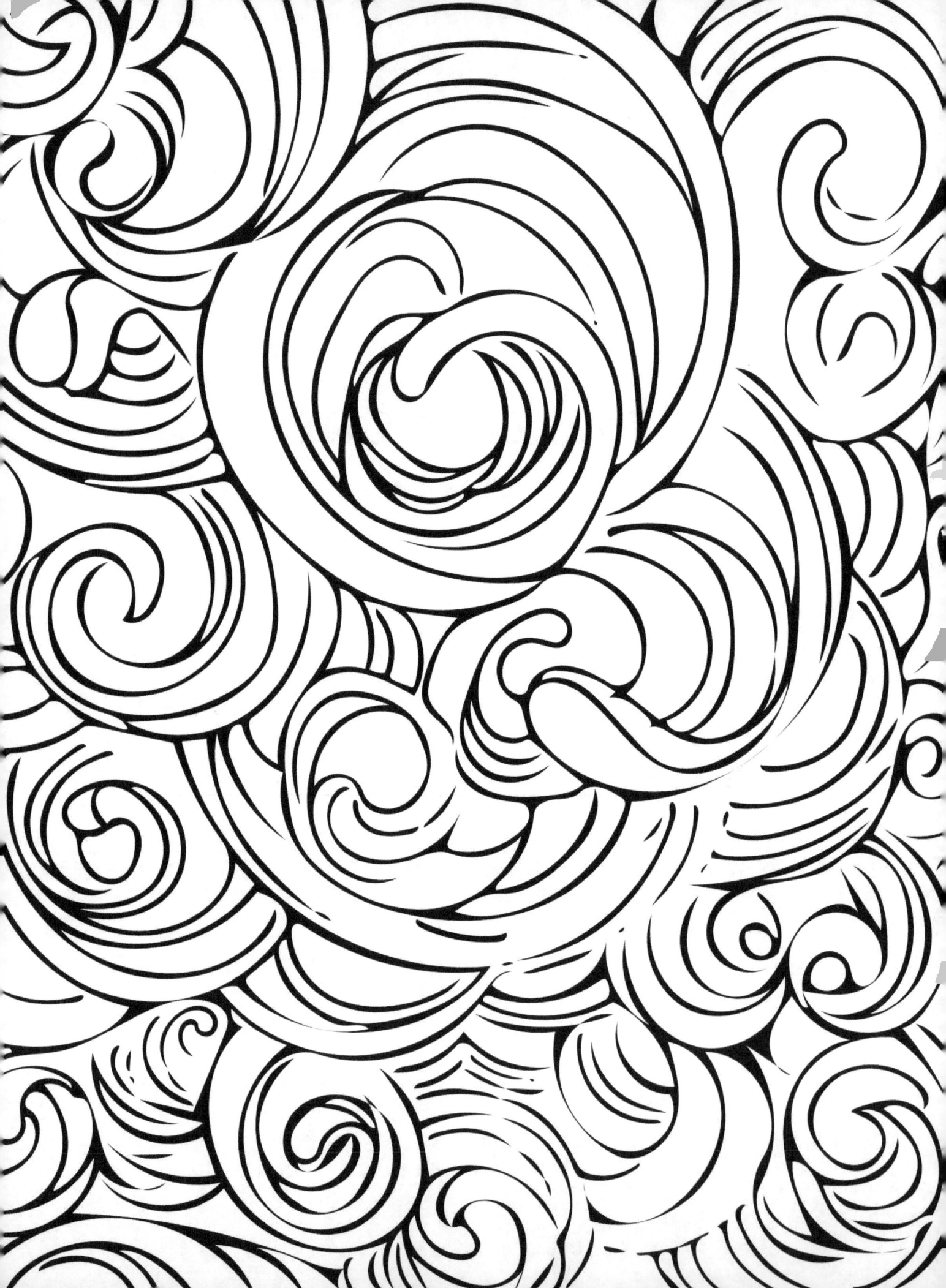

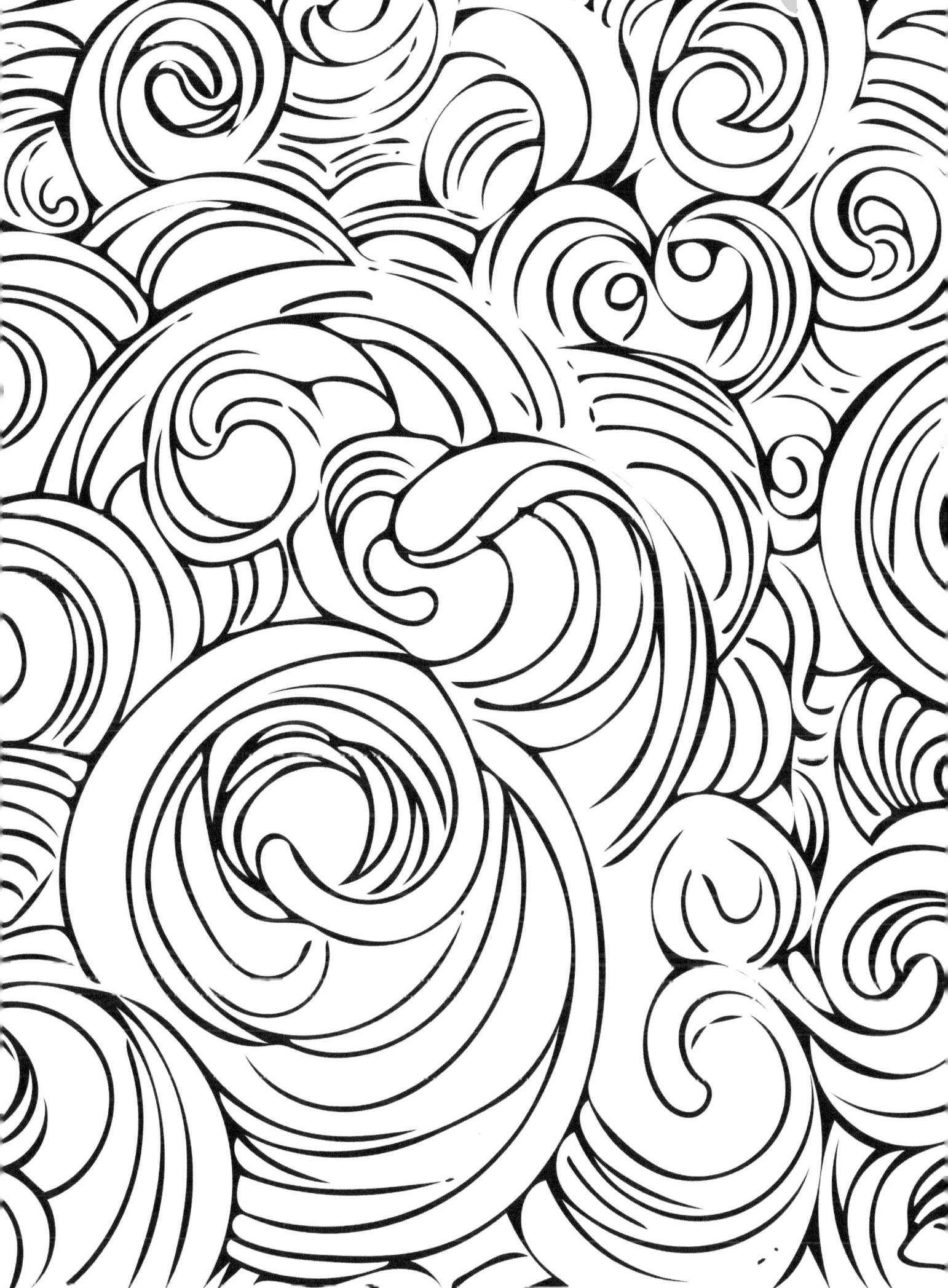

PROTECT OUR WATER

SIGNED:_____

PROTECT OUR
WATER

SIGNED:_____

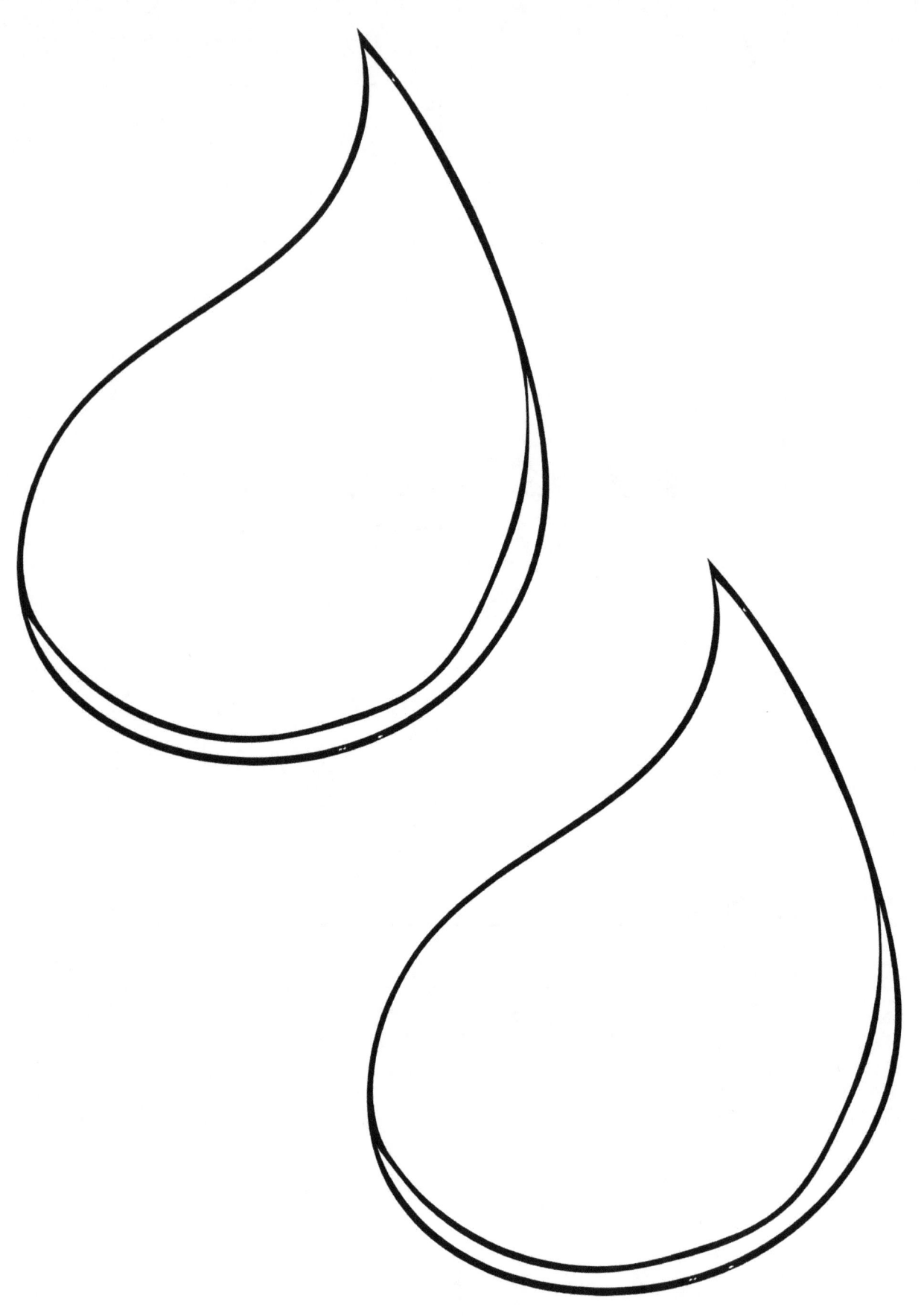

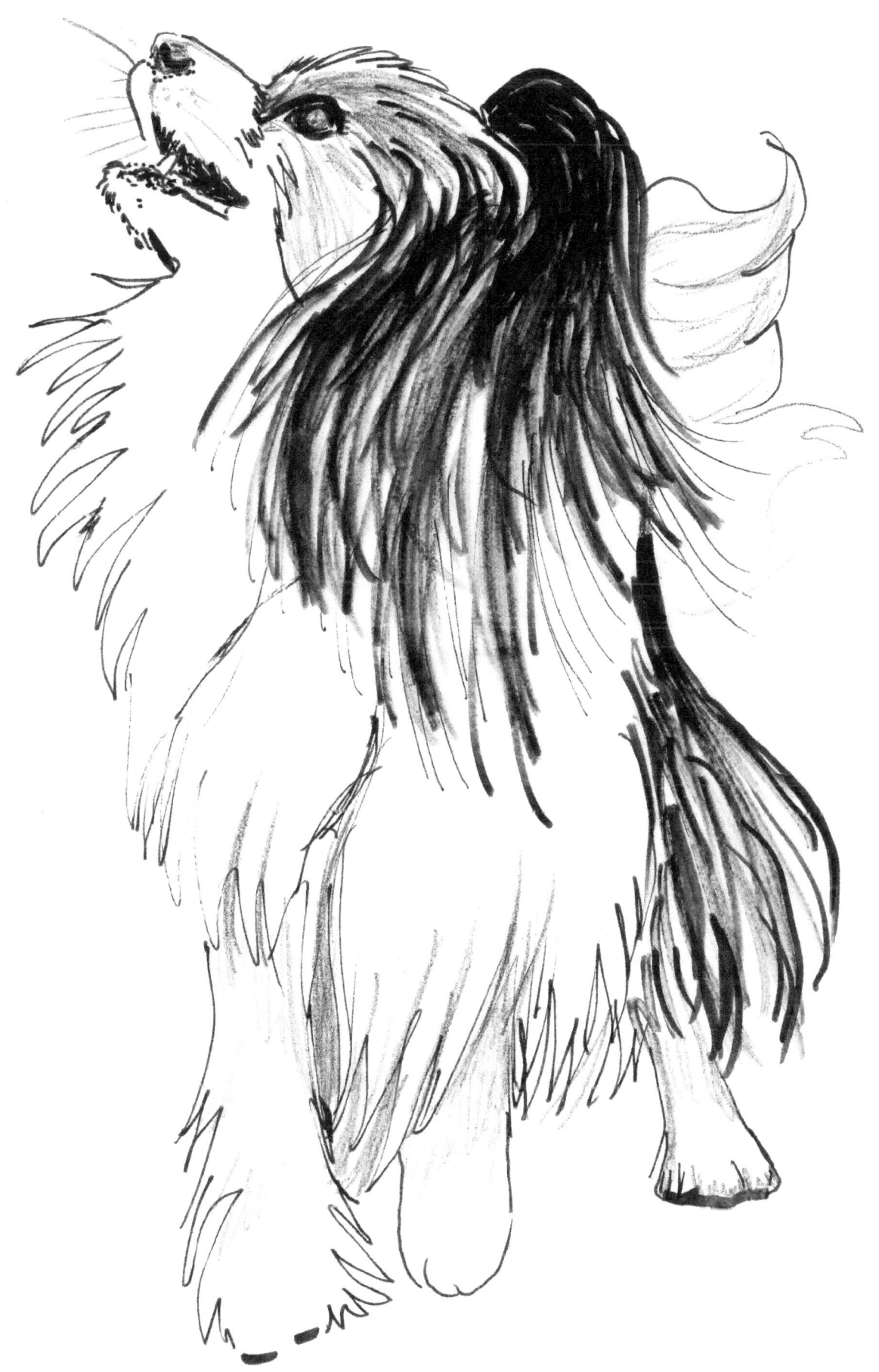

PROTECT OUR
WATER

SIGNED:_____

PROTECT OUR WATER

SIGNED:_____

PROTECT OUR WATER

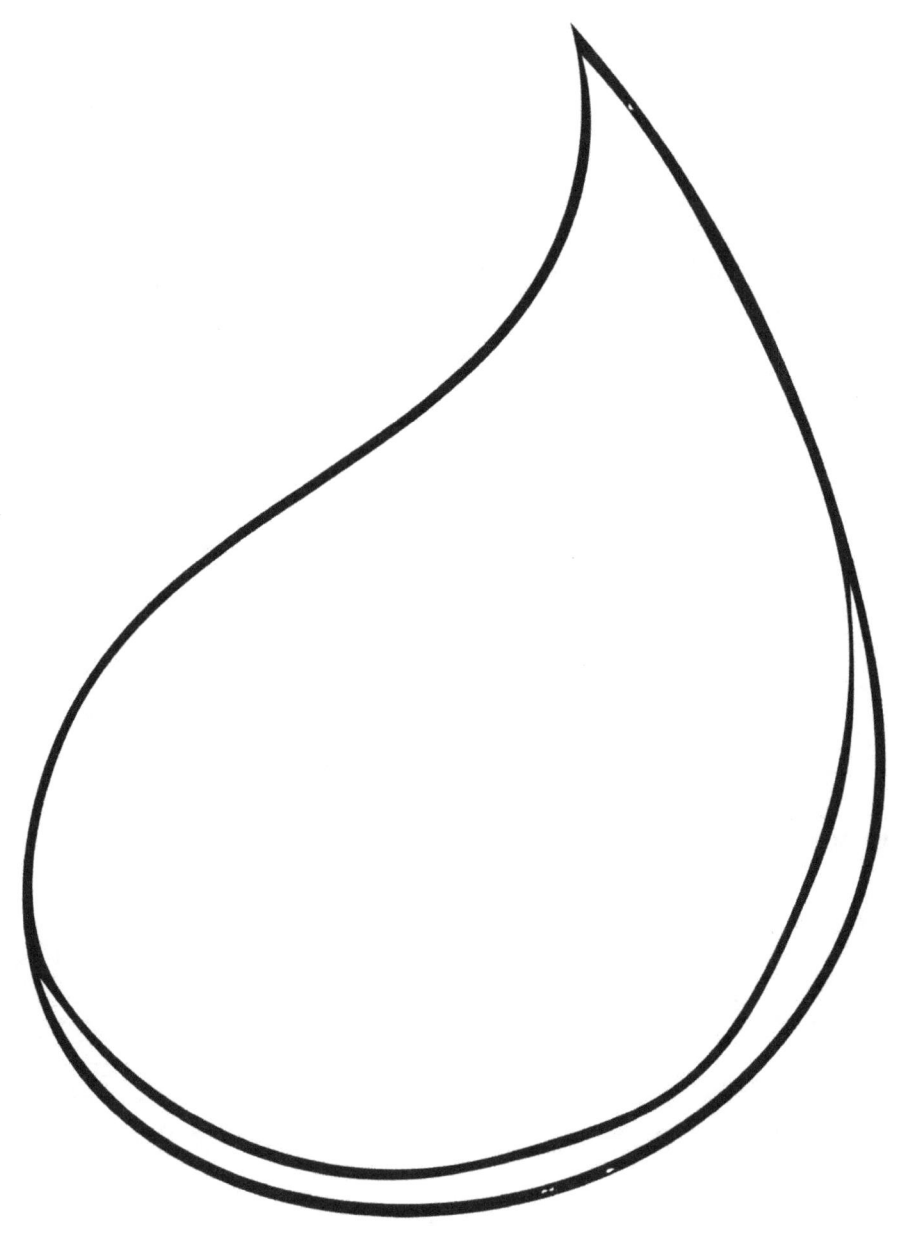

SIGNED:_____